Dealing with difficult people is one of the greatest obstacles we all face in life. You can be the right person, surrounded by the wrong people, and end up with the wrong results. In his new book, Pastor Mike Robertson shows us how to live an amazing life, even when surrounded by difficult people. His wisdom, stories, and humor make this great book a must-read for anyone who knows people.

—Tim Storey

celebrity life coach and author of *Comeback & Beyond*

My friend Mike Robertson has done a fine job in writing a very helpful book about dealing with difficult people. This is something all of us in ministry, business, and family have to face regularly. I believe this practical book could be a great resource in the hands of our pastoral, leadership, and business staff and teams, and save a lot of unnecessary time-wasting with people that we will just not win with. Relationships are the cause of every problem in the world, and we are either going to equip ourselves to be a part of the solution, or remain a part of the problem. This is an equipping book. Get it!

—André Olivier

senior pastor of Rivers Church in Johannesburg, South Africa and author of *Pain is Inevitable, Misery Is Optional*

Mike Robertson's readers have reason to be pleased with his new work, *Dealing With Difficult People*. Of particular relevance are the biblical examples and everyday life stories. It is essential that we understand the influence of Christ and Christian faith on our dealings with difficult people. One of the most significant reasons we were actually able to push beyond the difficulty and find the God-given reason for the existence of difficult people in our lives is revealed in Mike's book. If you have a difficult person, this book will help you. May we take his words to heart.

—Scott Wilson
lead pastor of Oaks Church in Red Oak, Texas
and author of *Parenting With Purpose: 7 Keys to Raising World Changers*

Mike has done it again. First it was *I Shook Hands with Death*, second was *Mind Viruses*, and now a masterpiece on how to deal with the difficult people in your life. Much of the way we interpret dealing with difficult relationships was formed by our worldview when we were young. Mike not only does a masterful job in addressing learning from early dysfunctional relationships but also reveals the hidden purpose difficult people play in forming our future. No one wants to do the heavy lifting anymore when it comes to relationships. This book is a must-read for anyone navigating the waters of difficulty. Christian and non-Christian readers alike will walk away with a conviction that difficult people were placed in our lives for a reason.

—Rich Wilkerson Sr.
senior pastor of Trinity Church in Miami, Florida and author of *I Choose Honor, The Key To Relationships, Faith and Life*

We live in a world of disrespect and dishonor. My friend Mike Robertson shows that without a download from heaven, the most important ingredients in dealing with difficult people will be missing. What a difference the gospel makes! Mike shows us through his experiences how a radical transformation and a near-death experience mentored him in dealing with difficult people. Great insights. Read this book and realize the importance and power of Christ in dealing with difficult people.

—Benny Perez
lead pastor of ChurchLV in Las Vegas, Nevada and author of *More: Discovering the God of More When Life Gives You Less*

DEALING

WITH

DIFFICULT

PEOPLE

WITHOUT KILLING THEM

MIKE D. ROBERTSON

Dealing With Difficult People (Without Killing Them)
copyright ©2020 Mike D. Robertson

ISBN: 978-1-950718-42-9

Printed in the United States of America

cover design by Joe Deleon

Avail
225 W. Seminole Blvd., Suite 105
Sanford, FL 32771

CONTENTS

DEDICATION

Dad, you didn't live long enough to read any of my books, but your butt kickings paid off! I didn't understand you when I was young; I do now, and I can't wait to see you in eternity. Thank you for all you did for me.

ACKNOWLEDGMENTS

The term "impostor syndrome" was coined in 1978 by two psychologists, Dr. Pauline Clance and Dr. Suzanne Imes. It refers to the feelings of inadequacy someone has despite evidence of their success. Basically, it's the fear that one day you will be "found out," that people will realize you are not all that smart.

I thank God for the fear of being found out. It propels me to work harder, dig deeper, and pray like a madman. Having said all that, there are four people who deserve the credit for any good that may come from this book. Without them, I really am just an impostor!

First and foremost, my two sisters and my niece. JoAnn Speakman has served alongside me as a researcher for years. She has helped me more times than I can count, finding interesting material. I could not have survived my speaking schedule over this past decade without her. And, actually, I used to hide in her home when I was running from a difficult person.

Second, Barbara Temples, my second sister. She helped me put together the first draft of this manuscript. Without her this book may not have happened. Plus, she gave me my first car, which made it easy for me to run away at fifteen when I was dealing with a difficult person in my life (more about that soon)!

Then there is my niece Caitlin Selvidge Caballero. She too has helped me over the past few years in research. I would say she is my favorite niece, but it would offend my other nieces. (However, she really is my favorite, and a wonderful mom.)

Last, there is Andy Butcher. He was the final writer who helped me put these words together. This book reads a lot better than I actually sound for one simple reason: Andy Butcher. Thank you, Andy, you made this journey an enjoyable one.

If any reward comes from this book, may heaven add it to these four's accounts.

—Mike D. Robertson
Visalia, California
March 2020

INTRODUCTION

The Hidden Blessings of a Jackass

THE BIGGEST JACKASS I ever had to deal with was named Jack, appropriately enough. He was a genuine four-legged, ornery jackass. Dad got him for when we needed to plow the earth on our tree farm in spaces where there wasn't enough room to maneuver machinery.

A jackass is the offspring of a male donkey and a female horse, bred for its compact size and strength. Jack made it possible for us to turn ground we could not otherwise have cultivated. But, man, could he be stubborn! We chained him up to make sure he didn't cause too much damage, but on occasion he would break free and go charging through the trees, stripping the bark from them.

Finally, Dad decided one day that Jack was more of a headache than a help. He sent him off to the glue factory. Much as he had been a pain in the neck, I cried for Jack the day he went away. That was partly because I had gotten used to his ways. And I also had to acknowledge that he had been a help to us.

I learned from Jack that sometimes you have to take the rough with the smooth. It was a lesson that helped me with my father, and many other difficult people since.

After fighting the Nazis in Europe during World War II, Dad came home from the army to West Texas, where my siblings and I became his little platoon. He was an unyielding drill sergeant who took no prisoners. Everything had to be done just so, or there would be big trouble.

Having grown up during the Depression and then experienced the horrors of war, he was determined that we were going to learn to take care of ourselves. But if his motivation was love, he sure had a strange way of showing it. Frankly, if anyone practiced his kind of parenting these days, their mugshot would be on the six o'clock news.

Dad had us work seven days a week in his trucking and grocery store businesses and help out around the nursery and landscaping businesses. Our efforts were never good enough. A brawler who would go down the street to pick a fight just for the fun of it, he also arranged them for me, to help toughen me up. And if any of us kids stepped out of line even a fraction, we would get a beating—all of us.

When it came to being difficult, Dad gave Jack a run for his money.

As the seventh youngest, I soon got tired of receiving a whipping for some infraction of one of my older brothers. One time, when I was about fifteen, I was so fed up of living under my father's hard hand that I ran away with two buddies. We jumped into my beat-up first car, an Oldsmobile, and headed out.

The transmission died in the hills of New Mexico and we were picked up as runaways. We spent a night in jail before returning home, defeated. I came back to West Texas knowing that if I was to survive, I had to find a way of dealing with the old man without setting him off. Instead of provoking conflict, I began to seek connection. By the time he died when I was just seventeen, he and I had developed some level of friendship where once there had only been enmity.

Decades later, I look back on my early years with mixed feelings. My father certainly had a lot of shortcomings, but from where I am now, I can also see the ways he shaped me for my future. I wouldn't be the man I am today—pastor, leader, husband, friend—without some of the lessons I learned from Dad. I often jest: God gave you a family to remind you there's a devil! But, he also gave them to grow us up.

Now, I'm not saying that being part of a family is all a bad thing, of course. But even the best, most godly families are flawed, because they are all made up of imperfect people. And most of us have suffered some sort of hurt in our families, at some stage, because of tough relationships.

We don't just have to deal with them at home. We are going to come across difficult people at work and in the community—even in the line at the grocery store. They are even there in church. Like that old poem says:

To dwell above with saints we love,
well that will be such glory;
but to dwell below with saints we know,
now that's a different story.

Everyone has to deal with difficult people at some stage in his or her life. But when you are in leadership you have to face them more frequently, by nature of your position and responsibility. It just comes with the job, whether you're a corporate executive, a church volunteer, or a parent!

Some of these challenging types seek you out because you're the one in charge, and they want you to know what they think. But on occasions, you have to step in when you see difficult people causing problems.

Uncomfortable as this is, the simple fact is that wherever we encounter them, difficult people can play an important part in our lives if we will let them. Sometimes we must face an adversary if we are to rise up to the next level God has for us, whether that's in church leadership, in business, or in our homes.

That was certainly true for David. Though he had been anointed king of Israel, there was someone else on the throne. Saul was so threatened by the young shepherd boy who played a mean harp that he tried to kill him by throwing a javelin at him. David had to run from the palace even though he was in line for the throne.

Something happened in the years that followed. His adversary, Saul, forced David to dig deep into his character, to forge something of steel that would prove crucial when he did finally reach the position that was rightfully his.

RUNNING FROM DIFFICULTY

The senior pastor at the church where I was hired on to do youth ministry as a young believer was a real old-school type. The boys in the church's Christian school had to wear long pants at all times—even when on the basketball court! Needless to say, by the third quarter they would be so hot they would be dragging. No wonder we never won a game against other schools.

Even though I'd be out until late at night with youth group activities, the pastor expected me to turn up for work at eight o'clock sharp the next morning. We were the only church I knew of where the staff had to punch a clock, and he told me if I was late he would dock my pay accordingly. Much as I chafed under all this, and people encouraged me to get out, I didn't feel it was right to leave. I hung in there and tried to serve him well. In due time we even became sort of friends. And looking back, I learned a lot from him about leadership—even if much of it comes under the category of what not to do!

However, most of us avoid difficult relationships if we can, for one reason or another. We don't like conflict, so we steer clear of or withdraw from people with whom we clash, if at all possible. Who needs that kind of negativity, right? Or we may run from a difficult relationship because we worry that it might reflect badly on us. They may think we are the problem!

The most common reason we run from difficult relationships, though, is probably because we have this secret belief that things should come easy. Instant answers to every question from Google, same-day delivery for online shopping, in some places. It's become part of the American way—forget sweat and effort, we get trophies just for showing up.

That sort of mentality has even crept into the church. So many Christians seem to think that salvation is some kind of Willy Wonka Golden Ticket giving them access to constant blessings. That has neither been my life experience, nor do I find it to be that way in the Bible.

Don't misunderstand me, life with God is good! He works miracles in and through us. He leads us into abundant life. But it isn't perfect, because we live in an imperfect world, marred by sin. With a large church, we have a funeral almost once a week. Among the services I led recently were one for a dear friend who took his own life, and another for a sweet teenage girl killed in a car wreck.

How can you make sense of things like that? There is no easy answer. And yet I am convinced that, because He is so creative and kind, God is somehow able to take and use even hard things—and hard people—for good.

WELCOMING AN ADVERSARY

Like David, Joseph faced adversaries on his way to his destiny. Some might argue that the first ones he faced—his brothers—were of his own making. When the teenage Joseph told his siblings about the dream he had, in which he was the moon and they were the stars, bowing down to him, they were not happy, to say the least.

They threw their kid brother into a pit, and then they sold him to some passing traders for twenty shekels of silver. Joseph's life was clearly going in the wrong direction! And his roller coaster ride continued when he arrived in Egypt.

First he found favor after being sold to Potiphar, Pharaoh's top guy. Pleased with his work, Potiphar put Joseph in charge of all his household, until Mrs. Potiphar took a liking to the young man and falsely accused him of attacking her because he resisted her advances. From there Joseph found himself thrown into prison, where he languished for some time before finally being freed and appointed to Pharaoh's side.

Each adversary and adversity along the way worked something deep in Joseph, helping mold him into the man who would rescue his brothers when they came to him in their time of desperate need—bowing before him just as he had spoken years earlier. Each situation ushered Joseph one step closer to his destiny.

It wasn't a quick and easy process. Joseph's journey from the pit to the palace took about fifteen years. But when he finally got to the place God intended, he was able to see the fruit of his difficulties. He called his first son Manasseh, meaning, "For the Lord has caused me to forget the trouble my family put on me." And his second child he named Ephraim, which means, "For the Lord has caused me to bear fruit in the land of my affliction." His sons were evidence that he could see the good that had come from his bad.

Joseph seems to have endured those years of struggle with great patience. He appears to have known something we need to learn when we face adversaries—that their time is limited. Sometimes all hell seems to break loose around us because the enemy knows that his time is running out, and he wants to have one more shot at discouraging or distracting us.

Among the devil's many weaknesses is that he is impatient. So if you can hang on and hang in there, he will eventually give up. Remember that in James 4:7 we are told, "Resist the devil, and he will flee from you."

Our greatest example in dealing with difficult people is Jesus, naturally. He faced opposition from his birth, when Herod tried to have Him killed. Jesus would eventually die at the hands of rulers, but not until God's appointed time. Ultimately, Jesus was betrayed by one of his inner circle, one of the disciples He had walked with and nurtured for three years. Not only that, but Judas used an intimate gesture, a kiss, to identify Jesus to the mob that had come to arrest Him at Gethsemane.

But consider this: Through his difficult relationship with Judas, Jesus would reach his destiny, the cross.

So how did Jesus greet his betrayer?

"Friend," He said, according to Matthew 26:50.

That is amazing. Even in this difficult encounter, Jesus could be welcoming, in a way.

There is a great lesson for us here. How do we handle the difficult people in our lives, who may be instrumental in our reaching the destination God has in mind for us, if we will let them? Will we accept them as part of God's process?

chapter one

ROOTED IN RELATIONSHIPS

I'M FORTUNATE TO live in Visalia, in the heart of California's San Joaquin Valley, pretty much midway between Los Angeles and San Francisco. It's a beautiful part of the country, known as the breadbasket of the nation for its rich agriculture. We're famous for our fruits and vegetables.

Less well known is that my area is a holding place for some of the toughest criminals around. Within an hour's drive of Visalia there are half a dozen state prisons, accounting for around 17,000 prisoners. The one at Corcoran is best known as the long-time home to cult leader and killer Charles Manson. It is a violent place:

Just in the last few weeks, one prisoner was murdered by a fellow inmate and another took his own life. Our church services are broadcast into these prisons, and I'm always getting letters from prisoners telling me they consider me to be their pastor.

Being in such close proximity to these institutions, we have a fair number of people in our church with experience of what it's like to be there, on either side of the bars. There are former prisoners who have started new lives on being released, and others they interacted with while incarcerated—guards and other prison staff, police officers, and attorneys. One of our members, Anthony, fed Manson his breakfast every day for years.

I have heard lots of stories of how brutal life can be inside. It's not really surprising. After all, while sadly some people are imprisoned unjustly, many inmates are there because, one way or another, they have proved to be difficult people. They have cheated or harmed others, put them at risk, or broken the law in some way.

Thankfully, that doesn't have to be the end of their stories. Those of us on the outside may not have broken federal or state laws like they did—or perhaps just been fortunate enough not to have gotten caught doing so! But, like everyone on planet Earth, we have broken God's law. We are all equally sinners in need of God's grace and forgiveness. Sometimes, it seems to me, people who have been convicted of crimes are more aware of how wonderful salvation is than folks who consider they have lived "good" lives.

But when you house a bunch of difficult people in the same place in tough conditions, there are going to be problems. And how does the criminal justice system handle the roughest and hardest who are in prison, the ones they cannot do anything with? It puts them in isolation.

This isn't just to keep everyone else safe. It is also supposed to punish and persuade troublemakers to straighten up, because being totally alone, cut off from human contact, is awful. After a time with only their own thoughts and their own company, people can start to go crazy.

Research has found that prisoners put in isolation have increased depression and anxiety, and also get more violent, not less.[1] They so long for even the smallest amount of interaction that they will go to extreme lengths, screaming incessantly or making their

1. Bennett, Kevin. "What Really Happens Inside Prisoner Isolation Cells." *Psychology Today.* https://www.psychologytoday.com/us/blog/modern-minds/201806/what-really-happens-inside-prisoner-isolation-cells. June 29, 2018.

cell toilet overflow, so someone has to come and check on them. Prison isolation can be so damaging that the United Nations has banned its use for juveniles and the mentally ill.

The takeaway from all this is simple: People, even difficult people, need people! This basic truth shouldn't surprise us—God created Adam in his image, which is a three-person relationship of Father, Son, and Holy Spirit. No wonder, then, that after putting Adam to work in the Garden of Eden, He declared, "It is not good for the man to be alone. I will make a helper suitable for him" (Gen. 2:18).

Whether we like it or not, we all need others, to help make us more like God intends for us to be. We have to be rooted in relationships with others if we are to really grow in God.

I get concerned when I see Christians who think they don't need to be in relationship with other believers. Their attitude seems to be, "I've got the Bible and the Holy Spirit, and that's all I need." To me, they are a heresy waiting to happen. None of us is so full of God that we get everything right. That is why the Bible describes the church as "the body of Christ." We are all part of each other and need all those other parts so that we can function properly.

Even tough-guy heroes need help: For the Lone Ranger it was Tonto; for Batman it was Robin!

HEALTHY RELATIONSHIPS, HEALTHY LIVES

There are all sorts of benefits of good relationships. Many studies have found a link between them and better health. One time, I heard author and speaker Henry Cloud at a conference where he told about a study back in the 1960s of the residents of Roseto, Pennsylvania, who were discovered to have a much lower incidence of heart attacks than other communities.

Researchers figured that maybe the secret was their super-healthy diet, only to find some of the worst eating habits in the country. Many of the folks there were Italian immigrants, eating lots of red meat and other fatty foods. They also liked to drink wine and smoke cigars. So much for the good-eating theory.

In time, those leading the study stumbled across the recipe for Roseto's healthy hearts. It turned out that most everyone there knew everyone else. Coming from the old country with a long history of community, they had continued to weave their lives together. As an article in *The Huffington Post* put it, "In short, Rosetans were nourished by people."[2]

Fast-forward to the 1990s, and things had changed in Roseto in a big way. Many of the older folks had moved away or passed on, and that close sense of community was no longer to be found. Along the way, the incidence of heart disease had risen to similar levels elsewhere.

Other research has found heightened happiness and a greater sense of well-being among people who say they have vibrant relationships with others. But the benefits aren't just emotional and physical, they can also be practical. People with friends get ahead in life. As Proverbs 27:17 says, "As iron sharpens iron, so one person sharpens another."

James McConchie, a researcher at Claremont Graduate University in California, observes that "people who are thriving are usually doing so with the help of others." Peak athletes have coaches and top executives have mentors, he points out.[3] "Even those contemplative Buddhist monks

2. Positano, Dr. Rock. "The Mystery of the Rosetan People." *The Huffington Post*. https://www.huffpost.com/entry/the-mystery-of-the-roseta_b_73260. March 28, 2008.

3. McConchie, James. "How Your Relationships Can Bring Out the Best in You." *Greater Good Magazine*. https://greatergood.berkeley.edu/article/item/how_your_relationships_can_bring_out_the_best_in_you. July 30, 2019.

who seem to be at the pinnacle of self-transcendence are almost always surrounded by other transcendent monk friends," he says.

He's right. The people around you are either making you better or they are pulling you backward. You just cannot go down to the bar or the frat house and hang out with all your beer bong buddies and expect some high-performance things to happen. This fundamental reality is part of the elevator speech I give to young people whenever I get the chance.

I don't mean I am making a sales pitch to them. I tell them that every day, they start out on the fifth level. They step into the elevator of life, and they get to make a decision: Do they want to go higher, or do they want to go lower? Remember, I say, that the best rooms are at the top of the building, while all the junk is kept below stairs! They can punch button 6, 7, or even 10, or they can choose 2, 1, L, or B.

They are free to decide, I tell them, but the direction they select will help determine where they find themselves in five years or ten. Will they be enjoying a corner office with a view or a penthouse, or grubbing around in the basement? Often, we avoid those higher-number buttons because we know the people up there are going to demand something of us in some way, while those below will likely just let us slide along without having to try too hard. Just because some people make us uncomfortable does not necessarily mean they are difficult; they just require more of us than we may want to have to give.

Simply put, if you want to become all God has in mind, you are going to have to be in life-giving relationships with other people—and that is going to include some difficult people, like it or not. But before we get to consider how to navigate the challenging ones, let's look at the other types of relationships we need.

It's important to know what to look for in relationships, because they are not all the same. Different people will enrich and encourage us in different ways, just as we need a balanced diet of food to enjoy the best health. An endless intake of soda and chips may seem enjoyable at the time, but there will be a price to pay down the road. In the same way, "easy" relationships won't meet all our needs.

I think back to when I was a teenager, hanging out with my buddies. We sure had some fun, but if I had just stayed with them, today I might be just the same as I was back then—drunk, high, stupid, or some combination of all three! Actually, given the downward spiral of sin, I may well be in prison myself, or even dead, but for God's intervention. I'm so glad that He got a hold of me before I could make too many more mistakes.

From my own life and through pastoring others over several decades, I have come to believe that we all need to have four different kinds of relationships in our lives.

FRIENDS FOR A REASON

Many folks seem to think that maturity comes naturally, just like gray hairs. But there is a big difference between getting older and growing up. The first is inevitable, no matter how many supplements you take. The second is optional. It only happens if you choose it.

The fact is, we all need help in growing up, and God often sends people to assist with the process. Our job is to recognize them, and make the most of what they have to offer. We need to be good students of the teachers God allows into our lives.

Chief among them are our families. It's in the home that we first start to learn about communication and affection, about care and conflict. Family is like boot camp for life, preparing us for what is ahead. For some of us, these are enjoyable lessons; for some of us they are painful.

One time, a young lady come to me for help, distraught about something her mother had said. "Pastor, she got mad at me and said she wished I'd never been born," the teenager told me through tears. "She said that if she had to do it all over again, she would not go through with the pregnancy, because she hated me being here."

Honestly, sometimes I despair of the dumb, heartless things people can say or do. I put my arm around that girl, and I told her, "Whoa, whoa, whoa. It doesn't matter how you got here. You're here! What matters is what you do now you are. It doesn't matter that your parents do not recognize that—matter of fact, God had to use their special DNA to get you together, and you're fearfully and wonderfully made in the eyes of the Lord."

While some people are only too happy to put their families behind them, others can want to cling on longer and tighter than they should. Don't misunderstand, I'm not anti-family in any way. But we can get things a bit out of balance, if we are not careful. In fact, sometimes the family can almost become something of an idol in different communities. I know of situations where people put their commitment to relatives above everything else, even involvement with a local church.

I'm not suggesting we treat our families lightly, but I do think some people confuse honor and obligation when it comes to relatives. They are not the same thing. We're called to honor our parents in the Ten Commandments, but that doesn't mean having to go home every Thanksgiving and Christmas.

Don't forget the account of the first marriage. After describing Adam and Eve's union, Genesis 1:24 says, "That is why a man leaves his father and mother and is united to his wife, and they become one flesh." The forming of a new family requires some measure of separation from the old one. This is important, because you cannot reach your tomorrow destinations if you are hanging on to all your yesterday associations. In some ways, you have to be prepared to let go of your history to be able to reach out and take hold of your destiny. Unfortunately, some people try to hold on to their past at the expense of their future.

Look at what happened when Abram didn't cut family ties as he should have done. After the death of Abram's father, Terah, in Haran, God told him, "Go from your country, your people and your father's household to the land I will show you" (Gen. 12:1).

Abram did set out from Ur of the Chaldeans, as he was told—but he took with him his nephew, Lot, whose father, Haran, had passed away. Did Abram feel like he had some sort of ongoing obligation to Lot because of his late brother, Haran?

Whatever, the reason, Abram's failure to make a clean break as he had been instructed resulted in all sorts of complications. He and Lot ended up falling out over the best grazing land for their flocks, ultimately going their separate ways. But when Lot and his family were later carried off by invaders, Abram still felt he had to come to the rescue.

Chances are if you have ever gotten together with extended family for Thanksgiving or Christmas or some other big holiday there has been some sort of tension, if not a blow-up. It may not be over whose sheep eat what, but who carves the turkey. Maybe Uncle Gerry got drunk again, or that long-simmering feud between your cousins over who makes the best pie erupted.

If that's been your experience, you are not alone: One study found 88 percent of respondents were stressed about celebrating the holidays. It also revealed that the average couple would have seven arguments during the season.[4]

I love my seven brothers and sisters. Growing up in a difficult home situation, we came through a lot together. Sort of like "battle buddies," we share a unique bond that will never change. But in the years since our childhood, we have grown and gone our separate ways. We keep in touch, and we would be there for one another in a heartbeat if there was a major need. But we don't live in each other's pockets. We have our own lives, shaped by some of what we learned together.

The old saying goes that blood is thicker than water. While that may be true, I also believe that the blood of Jesus which unites His followers should be the strongest tie. In God we become part of a bigger family.

FRIENDS FOR A SEASON

Visalia, where I live, isn't just deep in California's agricultural basin. It is also firmly part of "Raider Nation." When it's football time, there is a sea of silver and black all around declaring devotion to the now-Las Vegas Raiders.

---

4. Gervis, Zoya. "Holidays stress out 88 percent of Americans, study claims." *FoxNews.com.* https://www.foxnews.com/lifestyle/the-holiday-stress-out-88-percent-of-americans-study-claims. December 6, 2018.

The loyalty continues even after the team's recent relocation to the gambling mecca from their long-time Oakland home. Many fans make the four-hour drive from Visalia to the stadium for games.

The football season brings people from different backgrounds together over their shared passion and pursuit. It's the same in the rest of life. God brings people into our lives during seasons when we are in lock-step over something. It might be as work colleagues, or newlyweds, or couples with young children going through the same life stages, or some church ministry. Election time brings people together, campaigning for their candidate of choice.

Some people make deep connections with others during a period of great challenge or difficulty. Maybe they get to know each other through participating in some kind of a recovery group—addiction, or divorce, or bereavement. These can be really meaningful relationships, because of the depth of sharing that goes on. People get to see each other at their weakest and worst.

Because of that, things can go one of two ways as time goes by. Having "been in the trenches" together, some hold on to a strong sense of connection, even if they are not in much direct contact any more. For others, it's something they want to put behind them, because it's a reminder of a tough time in their lives they are glad to be able to put in the past.

Either way, seasons naturally come to an end. In both football and farming, there's a time for resting and renewing. Playing or plowing longer than you should isn't going to be beneficial in the long run. Some things need to come to an end before there can be more fruit.

Both friends for a reason and friends for a season are brought into our lives for a period that is finite, so what's the difference between the two, you may ask? Well, they do share some commonalities, and you might decide their nature changes over time. People can even move between the two.

However, to me there are a couple of distinctions. First, friends for a reason tend to come less by way of invitation. By that, I mean we have less choice about them—they are our family, they are our work colleagues. They are people we are stuck with for a time whether we like it or not! With friends for a season, we're more saying yes, please, than okay.

Then, friends for a reason have made some kind of a deposit in your life. They have brought something to you, maybe something they have directly taught you. Or they may have brought something out of you. Friends for a season, on the other hand tend to have a more indirect impact on your life; perhaps it is something you become aware of as you travel together for a while.

The thing about both kinds of friendship is that they can come with an expiration date on them, like a bottle of milk. I reached for one my wife, Karen, and I had left in the refrigerator when we went on a long trip, once, and found the use-by date was two weeks past. No problem, I thought; I'll just shake it up and everything should be okay. Boy, did I change my mind when I saw those curdled chunks bobbing around! I knew that if I popped the cap off, the mere smell would likely make me sick to my stomach. It was ready for the trash can.

That's the same with some relationships. They served their purpose, but you don't need to keep them around for ever. It's time to move on. It doesn't have to mean kicking people to the curb, but you do need to recognize that things are different between you now. Otherwise you end up holding onto unrealistic expectations that can cause hurt.

It's like this. If I am going away on a big trip, some folks might come to a special party before I leave. Others might come with me to the airport to wave me off. That's okay, because my destination is not theirs. Only a handful, if that, is actually going to board the plane with me.

These are the special people that go the distance.

FRIENDS FOR A LIFETIME

I call them my 2:00 a.m. people. These are the ones I could reach out to at that unearthly hour, knowing that they would answer when they saw my name come up on caller ID. And I know that, whatever I needed, they'd be there as soon as they could. I don't need all of both hands to count up these friends. But when you have some people like this in your life, you don't need many of them!

My experience is fairly typical. According to research, most people have around five others with whom they share what they consider to be an "intimate bond." Beyond that, they have fifteen "close friends," fifty "friends," and 150 "casual friends."[5]

Deep, committed friendships don't just happen, of course. They develop from friends for a reason and friends for a season. Often that season is college, when young people are

---

5. How many friends does the average person have? *GoodTherapy. com.* https://www.goodtherapy.org/blog/psychology-facts/how-many-friends-does-average-person-have-0208197. February 8, 2019.

figuring out life on their own for the first time. Something about exploring all those wide-open frontiers brings people together. I always encourage students to look for new friends when they go to school, because these relationships can be really formative. Even the roommate from hell can be used of God to help mature you!

Pain is a special kind of bond. When you have been through the fire with someone, you are knit together with them in a unique way. Think about the relationships that are forged between those who have served alongside one another in combat. Shared adversity is like a glue.

I am part of a small group of guys who have each other on speed-dial. We try to meet up for a few days at least once a year, just to hang out, catch up, and talk about whatever we need to. We call it Man Week, and it could be anywhere doing anything. Hiking, fishing, exploring some new place. There's really only one rule: guys only.

It's important to evaluate our relationships and consider which of these three categories they fall into. And keep in mind that it's a two-way street; God will use you as one of these kinds of friends in other people's lives, too. Having a sense of what He wants you to be for them is important.

Why the need for this sort of reflection on our relationships? Because without a clear understanding of what you should be expecting—to give or to receive—there is a lot of room for misunderstanding.

Think about some of the broken and bruised relationships you have heard about in church, or maybe experienced yourself. People are left feeling hurt after being let down in some way. It's understandable, because when you are involved spiritually with someone, you are connected at a deeper level than everyday friendship. When you get hurt there, you get really hurt.

But if you can identify that someone is in your life as a friend for a reason, you won't have the same expectations of him or her as you would a friend for a season, or a friend for a lifetime. These different kinds of relationships are like different bridges; they can bear different levels of weight. You wouldn't try to drive a fully-loaded truck over a gap that was spanned by just a couple of thin planks.

Unfortunately, some people can be a little naive when they go to church. They assume everyone there must love Jesus just like they do. But churches are full of all kinds of people, from sold-out saints to scheming sinners and everywhere in between. There are charismatic cougars and Pentecostal playboys! We need to be discerning.

I am not suggesting it means we should avoid everyone we are not sure about, though. In fact, some of those challenging or difficult people could be candidates for the fourth kind of relationship we need.

FRIENDS OF TREASON

Most of us wouldn't sign up for a Judas. Why let someone into your life knowing they are going to betray you? That just seems masochistic. Yet from Jesus' life we see that sometimes we have to deal with people who will let us down if we are to get to where God is leading us.

To start with, the three disciples He let into his innermost circle—Peter, and the brothers James and John—might be considered the most difficult of the bunch of twelve. Peter was the most impulsive and outspoken, but James and John ran him close. They didn't get the nickname "Sons of Thunder" for their peaceable personalities. Not only did they want fire from heaven rained down on the Samaritan town that didn't give Jesus a warm welcome (Luke 9), they also asked Him for VIP seating in heaven (Mark 10:37).

Jesus asked this trio to accompany Him when He wrestled in prayer in Gethsemane, the night He was betrayed.

They were the closest to Him of any human and they let Him down, falling asleep as He prayed for the strength to endure what was ahead.

To reach the cross, Jesus had to allow Judas into his life. It's not clear exactly at what stage in his ministry Jesus became aware specifically that Judas was the one who would sell Him out, but He certainly knew by the time He sat down for the Last Supper.

He told the disciples that one of them was going to betray Him. "Then Judas, the one who would betray Him, said, 'Surely you don't mean me, Rabbi?' Jesus answered, 'You have said so'" (Matt. 26:25). As I noted in the introduction, when Judas came back later that night with the crowd to arrest Jesus, He welcomed him as a friend—a friend of treason.

It's in the context of this web of different kinds of relationships that we get to deal with difficult people.

chapter two

YOU CAN'T KEEP RUNNING

I F YOU WANT the best answer to a question, it's good to go directly to the source. And when it comes to a biblical understanding of how to deal with difficult people, there may be no one better to turn to than the apostle Paul.

To start with, he had some insider knowledge on the topic. After all, he was the original difficult person himself! Before he became one of the leading figures of the early church, he was Saul, one of its greatest enemies. As people came to faith in Jesus in growing numbers after the Day of Pentecost, he played a major role in the efforts to snuff out the fledgling movement—Chief Bad Guy. Paul, as he became, is up there in Heaven's Hall of Fame.

But no one would have predicted that from his earlier years. He watched people's cloaks for them as they stoned Stephen for declaring the gospel before the Sanhedrin, and he gave a thumbs-up to the killing. Then he started going from house to house in search of believers, dragging men and women off to prison. In Galatians 1:13, he wrote of how intensely he "persecuted the church of God and tried to destroy it."

Bear that in mind the next time you find yourself dealing with a difficult person: God has the power to intervene and turn that life around! And it can happen in an instant. Saul didn't warm up to Christians over time. He was on his way to Damascus to round up more of the saints and lock them up when God intervened dramatically. Blinded by a bright light, Saul heard God speak to him personally.

Saul's bad reputation clearly went before him. When God spoke to Ananias, one of the believers in Damascus, and told him to go and pray for Saul so that his sight might be restored, Ananias wanted nothing to do with the assignment. "Have you not been watching the news, God?" Ananias sort of asked. Give him his due, though, he did eventually do what he was told. And when he got to where Saul was staying,

Ananias's first words of greeting were, "Brother Saul." It's worth remembering: Whatever differences we may have with or reservations we might have about another believer, that person is first and foremost our brother or sister in Christ. Part of a family.

WE ARE ALL WORKS IN PROGRESS

Paul's conversion was dramatic, of course. He went from persecutor to preacher overnight. Instead of hunting down Christians, he went to the synagogue to tell other Jews about Jesus. He was consumed by his great love for God. But he could still be difficult, at times.

Like him, we are all works in progress. As Paul wrote in 1 Corinthians 3:18, we are all "being transformed into his image with ever-increasing glory, which comes from the Lord, who is the Spirit." It's just that some of us have a lot more work that needs to be done than others!

For instance, so passionate was Paul in his mission that he didn't have a lot of patience with others. In part, Paul owed his ministry to Barnabas, who had championed him when others in the early church were wary of the former persecutor. The two men had teamed up for a missionary journey on which they took Barnabas's cousin, John Mark. But this younger man bailed on them along the way, ticking

Paul off. When Barnabas later suggested to Paul that they take John Mark along on their next trip, Paul was having none of it. In fact, their disagreement was so heated that Paul and Barnabas went their separate ways—the dynamic duo split up.

Many years later, a brief mention in one of Paul's letters indicated that perhaps he had eased up a little. "Get Mark and bring him with you," he wrote then, "because he is helpful to me in my ministry" (2 Tim. 4:11). His attitude toward John Mark seemed to have softened with time.

Then there was the occasion Paul called out Peter in public. He rebuked the famous apostle for giving in to pressure from others in the church who believed converts needed to embrace Jewish ways and pulling away from some of the Gentile converts. Paul didn't try to play nice, or gloss over what he saw to be Peter's wrong. Writing about the situation in his letter to the Galatians, he referred to Peter's "hypocrisy." Paul didn't sweep the difficulties under the rug.

Fact is, sometimes those we dismiss as "difficult" may just make us uncomfortable because we don't like to create a stir. Before we rush to pigeonhole people as awkward, we might do well to check whether that's really fair. Maybe they are just a bit bolder than we are.

The gospel fire in Paul's belly never went out from the day it was lit as he lay blinded on the Damascus road. His greatest passion was telling others about the incredible love of God which had stopped him in his tracks. However, he did mellow in some ways as he got older.

I've noticed the same kind of thing in my life: Principles remain important, but people are a much higher priority. I have learned to temper my zeal over the years some, too. I am no less passionate about telling people about God's love. I just recognize that people are different and not everyone warms to high-intensity interaction. Untamed enthusiasm can be counter-productive. It's like fire in the woods. Controlled burns are good; in fact, they help bring new life by re-balancing the ecosystem. But a careless forest fire can cause untold destruction, as thousands of people in California have experienced in recent times. "Consider what a great forest is set on fire by a small spark," says James 3:5.

As a young believer, I was determined to use every opportunity to share the gospel—even if it wasn't really an opportunity! I remember getting kicked out of a family celebration once because I wouldn't shut up about their need for God. Sometimes when this sort of thing happens we like to frame it as persecution, but as I look back it was really more because I was just a pain.

I also used to go witnessing door to door. On one of my excursions, I met a man who told me that he had a gun and if I ever went back to his door, he would use it on me. I decided it would not be wise to return. Over time, I learned to tone things down a little bit and be more sensitive. I realized that maybe I wasn't right all the time.

Under house arrest in Rome toward the end of his life, Paul had time to reflect on what really mattered. He had been around the block a few times by then. He had witnessed God's power in action, and he had experienced great personal hardship. The letters he wrote from his prison cell to some of the churches he had planted were among his most pastoral. They included one to the church in Philippi, in which he emphasized the importance of unity and love between believers as an example to the world around them.

As part of that, he called out two women in the congregation over a disagreement that had clearly become a source of disunity. "I plead with Euodia and I plead with Syntyche to be of the same mind in the Lord," he wrote (Phil. 4:2).

We don't know what these sisters had fallen out over. Judging by present-day church life, it could have been anything from design to doctrine—from the color of the drapes in the fellowship hall to whether or not the gifts of the Holy Spirit are revocable. Whatever the cause of the rift, there was clearly a conflict that was affecting the rest of the church, and Paul knew that it needed to be addressed.

LEADERS HAVE TO STEP UP

As a leader, Paul knew that it was not healthy to let difficult people continue in their ways without dealing with the problem. It remains true: We can't afford to ignore difficult people just because we are not directly involved or affected. They will have a negative impact on others we are responsible for, if we just leave things as they are. This is one reason anyone in leadership will have need to know how to deal with difficult people.

If you hear a weird knocking noise coming from your car engine, the answer isn't just to turn the radio up to drown it out. That may let you get a little farther down the road without having to acknowledge the problem, but sooner or later you are going to end up pulled over with smoke coming out from under the hood. And what might have just been a broken hose that needed replacing has now become a seized engine that's good only for the scrapyard. There's no point moaning about it then:

As a leader, you don't get to complain about what you tolerate.

Leaders are responsible for the culture in their churches, their organizations, or their families. If you allow toxic people to continue in their ways without addressing them, you will see that spirit infect others. That's why Paul offered this caution in 1 Corinthians 5:6, "Don't you know that a little yeast leavens the whole batch of dough?" Whether we like it or not, there are occasions when we have to step in.

It wasn't only in Philippi that Paul saw difficult people who needed to be handled. Sometime later, while still in prison in Rome, he sat down to write to another of the early churches, this one in Colossae.

Usually, Paul dictated his letters to an assistant. Sometimes he would pick up a quill to write a few words in his own hand, as if to assure the recipients that it really was he who was writing. He started his second letter to the church in Thessalonica this way, "I, Paul, write this greeting in my own hand, which is the distinguishing mark in all my letters." Toward the end of his letter to the Galatians (6:11), he told them, "See what large letters I use as I write to you with my own hand!"

Paul made the same sort of reference in his letter to Philemon ("I… am writing this with my own hand") and the members of the church in Colossae. Some scholars believe that he actually penned the whole thing personally. It's certainly short enough—less than 400 words in the original Greek—and personal enough for that to be the case.

Not only is Philemon the shortest of Paul's letters, it is also the only one directed first and foremost to an individual rather than a group of people—though he does include others in his "CC": Apphia, Archipus, and the rest of the members of the church. Interestingly, it is also the only one of Paul's letters that does not mention the cross and the resurrection.

In its few sentences there is some helpful guidance for anyone having to deal with difficult people. After opening with his greeting, he tells how he remembers Philemon and the others thankfully for their faith and their love for God's people, and how encouraged he has been by the way Philemon has been a blessing to others.

With that said, he gets down to business in verses 8-24:

I always thank my God as I remember you in my prayers, because I hear about your love for all his holy people and your faith in the Lord Jesus. I pray that your partnership with us in the faith may be effective in deepening your understanding of every good thing we share for the sake of Christ. Your love has given me great joy and encouragement, because you, brother, have refreshed the hearts of the Lord's people.

Therefore, although in Christ I could be bold and order you to do what you ought to do, yet I prefer to appeal to you on the basis of love. It is as none other than Paul—an old man and now also a prisoner of Christ Jesus—that I appeal to you for my son Onesimus, who became my son while I was in chains. Formerly he was useless to you, but now he has become useful both to you and to me.

I am sending him—who is my very heart—back to you. I would have liked to keep him with me so that he could take your place in helping me while I am in chains for the gospel. But I did not want to do anything without your consent, so that any favor you do would not seem forced but would be voluntary. Perhaps the reason he was separated from you for a little while was that you might have him back forever—no longer as a slave, but better than a slave, as a dear brother. He is very dear to me but even dearer to you, both as a fellow man and as a brother in the Lord.

So if you consider me a partner, welcome him as you would welcome me. If he has done you any wrong or owes you anything, charge it to me. I, Paul, am writing this with my own hand. I will pay it back—not to mention that you owe me your very self. I do wish, brother, that I may have some benefit from you in the Lord; refresh my heart in Christ. Confident of your obedience, I write to you, knowing that you will do even more than I ask.

And one thing more: Prepare a guest room for me, because I hope to be restored to you in answer to your prayers.

Epaphras, my fellow prisoner in Christ Jesus, sends you greetings. And so do Mark, Aristarchus, Demas and Luke, my fellow workers.

Before we unpack some of the lessons for us in all this, let's be clear about the three people involved in this situation.

Paul. The fiery apostle who carved a path for the gospel through much of the known world. Locked up in Rome but far from shut up. He preached to the Romans guarding him, and made an impact far beyond the walls within which he was confined. In his letter to the Philippians (4:22), he referred to believers who "belong to Caesar's household," probably as a result of his ministry to them. That's like there being born-again staffers at the White House or in England's Buckingham Palace.

Onesimus. A slave from Colossae, he fled his owner and somehow made his way to Rome, some seventeen hundred miles away. That suggests he had some street smarts and some strength of character. The text also alludes to the fact that he may have stolen something on his way out the door. It's not clear when and how he became a Christian—maybe it was on the journey. Maybe it was when he arrived in Rome. But somehow he came into contact with Paul, who took him under his wing and discipled him.

Philemon. We don't know how he and Paul connected; Paul never actually visited Colossae. The church there had been planted by one of Paul's apprentices, Epaphras, but clearly Philemon and Paul had come to know each other well somehow. Though he held slaves, Philemon enjoyed a good reputation.

It's worth noting that each of these three men was in prison one way or another. For Paul, it was literal imprisonment.

Ironically, though, he was probably the most free of all of them. His movements were restricted, yes, but no one could keep him from soaring in his relationship with Jesus. I am pretty sure he often sang praises to God, just like he did when he was jailed in Philippi with Silas one time (Acts 16).

Whenever I am talking to inmates, I always tell them that they may be incarcerated physically, but they don't have to be incarcerated spiritually. I encourage them to follow the example of Paul. Fall in love with Jesus, like he did, develop a deep relationship with God, and while you may be locked up in your circumstances, you will be as free as a bird in your spirit.

For Onesimus, freedom was fragile. As long as he remained a runaway slave, there was a price on his head. Bounty hunters were on the lookout for fugitive slaves, and it was illegal to help out runaways. Those who were caught could be beaten, branded, and even killed. Onesimus's past was never far away.

We don't know the details of what happened. Was Philemon a hard taskmaster who made life simply unbearable for Onesimus? Or was Onesimus just fed up with being forced to follow someone else's orders? Philemon had a good reputation, but maybe he harbored resentments against

Onesimus. If Philemon had been a fair master, Onesimus's running away may have made him look bad in the eyes of people who wondered if he had mistreated Onesimus.

Whatever the facts of the situation, we can be sure that each of them thought the other person was difficult.

A TIME TO RUN AWAY

Most of us have run away from something at one time or another. A situation or a certain someone seems to be too much, and the only solution we can come up with is to put some distance between us and it or them.

Chances are God will have us go back to work things out at some stage, when we have gained the grace or the strength or the wisdom or whatever else it may be we lack to deal with the situation and circumstances. But for the time being, separation might be a good thing.

That is certainly the case when it comes to domestic abuse and violence. If you are in a relationship where you are being mistreated, then you need to get away from there. While you are called to love and forgive your spouse, it does not mean you have to stay in a situation where he or she gets to harm you emotionally or physically or sexually. I've heard too many stories of pastors who have told wives they need to submit to their husbands, condemning them to further harm. My counsel to all who are fearful for their safety or for that of their children is to get out.

Maybe in time, with counseling for all involved, that relationship can be put back together. God's heart is always for restoration, but sometimes it just isn't possible. It takes both parties in a broken relationship to want to see it renewed.

Some kinds of running away are pretty obvious. The woman fleeing an abusive husband. The teenager leaving a neglectful home. Maybe it's someone who wants to break free from an addiction to alcohol or drugs, knowing they have to stop hanging around the people they have been partying with, even move away somewhere else.

Other times, we don't realize we have been running away until we look back to where we have come from and see our footprints. Like my friend and co-writer Andy Butcher, who served with a missionary organization for many years. Brought up in a non-Christian home, when he met Jesus as a young man it brought him into conflict with the values he had been raised with. Rather than pursue the career he had begun, he decided that he wanted to serve God full-time in some way.

Praying for direction and reading his Bible one night, Andy turned to Matthew 7:7-8, "Ask and it will be given to you; seek and you will find; knock and the door will be opened to you. For everyone who asks receives; the one who seeks finds; and to the one who knocks, the door will be opened."

This was a three-step process for people searching for the new thing or place God has for them, Andy decided. Ask God for an address, then seek it out, and then pray for the door to be opened. So he closed his Bible, knelt down, and asked God to send him an address.

The very next day, he received a letter in the mail from a missionary leader with whom he'd had some contact. In his letter, this missionary leader asked Andy whether he would come work with him in another country. Needless to say, Andy was pretty blown away by the fast answer to prayer. Think about it: The letter was already on the way when he prayed.

The rest of the story didn't play out so smoothly. It took two years of "seeking" and then "knocking" before Andy finally made it to the mission field. That time was full of testing to see how serious he was about wanting to do what he believed God was calling him to. But when he and his family arrived in their new homeland, he knew without a shadow of a doubt that God was leading him.

Here's the unlikely postscript, though: Many years later, Andy looks back on that whole series of events a little differently. He's still as sure as ever that God was in all that happened. However, with the benefit of a bit more wisdom and life experience, he also sees some other things going on. Though he didn't recognize it at the time, he now sees that a part of him was running away—from his family, his old life, his old ways. It's amazing how God can use even our confused and mixed motives to bring about His good purposes.

It might be that you need to run from people who want to hold you back, who want to hold you down. Their opinion of you might be suffocating.

Jesus experienced this. After teaching and healing the sick, He went back to His hometown with His disciples. He spoke in the synagogue, and the people were blown away by what they heard. However, some of them took offense and kind of trash-talked about Him. "Isn't this Joe the carpenter's kid? Who does he think he is, coming round here like he is someone special? Who does he think he is—God?"

The consequences of their attitude was significant. Mark 6:4-5 says, "Jesus told them, 'A prophet is not without honor except in his own town, among his relatives and in his own home.' He could not do any miracles there, except lay His hands on a few sick people and heal them. He was amazed at their lack of faith."

GRACE SETS US FREE

If you are in a place where people know your history, they can keep you from your destiny. They keep reminding you of some dumb decision you may have made back in the day. And let's be honest, who of us hasn't done something regrettable at some stage?

Because of our proximity to all the prisons, I am constantly reminded that there are people paying a lifetime's price for a moment's stupidity. I'm not suggesting there shouldn't be a consequence for crime, especially when it harms other people, but we need to be careful about judging people too quickly. That saying, "There but for the grace of God go I"? In my case, it's literally true.

In the summer of my senior year, I was at a party with a bunch of friends when one them, another Mike, suggested we see how fast I could get my 1970 Dodge Super Bee to go. With a belly full of beer, that seemed like a great idea, so he and I jumped in and took off.

I got it up to about 100 mph as we reached the edge of town, where I threw it into neutral to coast through and then picked up speed again when we came out the other side. We were doing about 70 mph when a car pulled out in front of us from a side street. I slammed on the brakes and they locked, sending us sliding into the oncoming vehicle.

Don't ask me how, but I walked away without a scratch. Mike was not so lucky: A star pole vaulter tipped for the state championships, his athletic career was over in a T-bone moment. The first responders had to use the jaws of life to prize him out of the wreckage. I may have been uninjured, but things could have ended differently if the police hadn't kept Mike's father from me when he arrived at the scene. If looks could kill, I'd have been a dead man.

Mike ended up in hospital for weeks with a fractured pelvis among his other injuries. I felt terrible. When he was finally discharged, I borrowed my father's truck and used it to take Mike wherever he needed to go, throwing his wheelchair in the back. I felt that I had to try to repay him somehow.

Mike's dad was prevented from getting his hands on me the night of the crash, but eventually he went after me. My blood-alcohol level had been way over the limit, and I found myself slapped with a charge of attempted vehicular manslaughter. I was facing possible serious prison time.

Then Mike's mom spoke up. She said that she couldn't press charges. "He's a Mike and I have a Mike," she said. "It was Thelma's [my mom] Mike who did this, but it could easily have been my Mike that did it to him." I walked away free that day because of the grace Mike's mom extended to me.

When people begrudge us something, they can hold us back. When they extend grace, they can let us go to become more of who we were meant to be. If Mike's mom had insisted on obtaining justice rather than offering mercy, I may never have gotten into the ministry through which I have had the privilege of leading thousands to Christ. Extending grace to a difficult person can produce unexpected results.

The way Mike's mom handled her difficult person, me, has borne fruit neither she nor I could ever have imagined. May God give Mike and his parents some of my rewards in heaven!

THE KEY TO ANSWERED PRAYERS

Forget how many Bible verses you can quote, or how often you attend church. The real measure of your faith is how you deal with difficult people. What do you do when you have been wronged in some way? When you feel that anger rising in you—over the way your roommate skipped out, leaving you to pay all the rent, or how your ex betrayed you. Forgiveness is the key. If we harbor unforgiveness toward people, we hinder God's ability to work in our lives in different ways.

First, it weakens our prayers. When Jesus taught what we call The Lord's Prayer, He made it clear that we are forgiven our sins as—in other words, to the extent that—we forgive people who have sinned against us. And why is that so important? Because in James 5:16 we read that "The prayer of a righteous person is powerful and effective."

I'm guessing that we'd all like our prayers to be powerful and effective, right? This passage tells us that this is true for a righteous person. That doesn't mean someone who is a good person in terms of behavior. It means in terms of being right with God, having all their sins forgiven—having His righteousness. And for that to be fully possible, we have to forgive others.

God will send someone into your life to test where you are in your relationship with Him. Jesus died for all our sins, and you can't forgive this person that one thing he or she did? That is why I always try to be sure I am not holding onto resentment.

Recently I got a call from someone I'd pastored twenty years ago. He loved God and thought he might become a preacher, but he had two serious weaknesses: women and money. "You need to get those two under control, my brother, or they are going to get you," I had warned.

Sadly, I was proved right. He got involved with some ladies whose tastes were richer than he was. To try to come up with more money he began gambling, but he was only getting into more debt. One day, he was so desperate he took an IRS refund check that had been sent to his roommate and cashed it. Then he just disappeared.

That was the last anyone had heard of him until he called me out of the blue not long ago.

"Hey, I need you to forgive me, Pastor," he said.

"For what?" I answered. I wanted to see what he might admit to.

"You know," he said. "All those things I did."

"Yes, I know."

"Would you forgive me?'

He sounded surprised when I told him, "I forgave you the week you did it."

"Really?" he said. "I've been carrying all this around for twenty years."

A TIME TO RETURN

Running away isn't a long-term solution. While it might be right for us to put distance between us and someone or something at a certain stage, likely there will come a day when it is time to go back.

Like when I tried to get out from under my father's harsh rule. My escape to New Mexico wasn't much longer than twenty-four hours, but it gave me enough space to realize something had to change. I went back determined to deal with my Dad situation.

I knew that I couldn't change him, but I could change the way I interacted with him. Recognizing that he was a top-down, military kind of guy, I realized there was no point trying to take him head-on. Better to learn to negotiate. I'd offer to help with one of his projects if he would help me maintain my car. We worked alongside each other, and just spending time in each other's company brought some of the tension down.

I tried to encourage my siblings to take a similar tack. "Don't go looking for a fight," I'd tell them. Like the time one of them overheard Dad telling one of his friends a tall tale. My brother piped up, "That's a lie." You can imagine that did not end well, for all of us.

I knew trying to engage my Dad was a bit of a gamble, but I had nothing to lose, and it panned out in the end. For Onesimus, going back to Colossae meant taking a risk. We don't know how long it had been since he had fled Philemon. It could have been that Philemon had forgotten all about it, or perhaps he thought about the servant that got away each and every day, and got angrier and angrier.

Imagine that Philemon had put Onesimus's rebellion behind him. Then, one day, he turns up on his doorstep. He wouldn't have known that a difficult person was coming into his life to test him. The same may be true for us: Perhaps God is sending someone we have put out of our minds back into our lives, to test us. How will we respond when that person shows up?

Either way, Onesimus didn't know how Philemon felt about him. He knew that Paul had put in a good word for him, but there was no guarantee things would work out. Philemon had every right to make Onesimus pay. Onesimus had to put himself at the mercy of his difficult person.

Going back is risky. It means opening yourself to rebuke or rejection. You may end up with egg on your face, but it's the right thing to do.

Not long after I became a Christian, I knew I had to go back somewhere. It was to the shoe store where I'd stolen a nice-looking pair of cowboy boots a couple of years earlier. This had been an unusual action for me; I may have been a hardcore partier, but I wasn't a thief.

The Holy Spirit had been working on my conscience ever since I'd gotten saved. I tried to give the boots away, but no one would take them, even though they were high quality. Finally, I just threw them out and went back to the store.

I told the people there what I had done, that I had become a Christian that I was sorry, and that I wanted to pay them back double. It took some persuading, but they eventually accepted the money. I left feeling so much lighter, knowing I had faced my past.

SETTING AN EXAMPLE

As leaders, sometimes we have to deal with difficult people publicly because there is a lesson for others to learn. Paul could have tried to resolve the issue between Philemon and Onesimus privately, just the three of them, but he saw it as an important issue for the whole church.

Not long after I arrived at Visalia First, I was surprised by how the church was struggling financially. For a fairly large congregation, we should have been much healthier.

Imagine how shocked we were to discover that a long-time member of the staff had been embezzling money for years and years—to the tune of around two million dollars.

When the news broke, I was advised to hold a press conference to handle all the media inquiries. I stood in front of what felt like a sea of cameras and microphones in the church youth center. The journalists wanted to know if I was mad at the person. I told them that desperate people did desperate things, sometimes. I said that we loved the person involved and her family, and that we had forgiven her. The journalists seemed kind of disappointed that I wasn't vengeful.

Later, when the woman concerned was sent to prison, we offered her daughter a scholarship to go to college.

BEING AN INTERMEDIARY

As leaders, we sometimes need to broker peace in a relationship where there is a difficult person—if not two! Like Paul, we may be able to use our relationship as lubricant to avoid sparks.

Paul appealed to Philemon on the basis of the love shared between them. Paul dropped a pretty big hint that, if for no other reason than he was in Paul's debt, Philemon should forgive and forget.

In our relationships with others, there are times when we can appeal for "some benefit… in the Lord" from them, as Paul tells Philemon in verse 20. It's not a question of quid pro quo. It's about the mutual blessing of being part of the body of Christ, giving and receiving.

In any kind of close relationship with another believer who is walking with Christ, there should be something you receive from their own relationship with Jesus. That's something I make a point of emphasizing to young people when they are dating. Your guy or gal may look good and smell sweet, but do they stir your heart for Jesus or just your hormones?

Not long after I got saved as a young man, I started dating this sweet little Baptist girl. Man, could she sing. I was convinced that if I could just get her to marry me, my life would be perfect. But as we began to spend more time together, I realized that something was missing. She had an angel's voice, but she wasn't as passionate about Jesus as I was. Finally, I had to sit her down one day and tell her, "You know what? If we are going to go together we have to grow together, and I don't see that happening. If you don't want to grow with me, you can't go with me."

We don't know how Onesimus's return to Philemon played out, but I would love to have been a fly on the wall for that meeting! We do know, however, that their relationship was restored, and the results for God's kingdom were good.

According to tradition, Onesimus went on to become the pastor of the church in Ephesus after Timothy. Later he was appointed the Bishop of Byzantium, which is present-day Istanbul. He is revered as a saint by some denominations. All this was achieved by someone once considered "useless," who got to live up the true meaning of his name, "beneficial." The runaway became revered. What a great reminder that it doesn't matter where you start out, it's all about where you finish. And all because Paul stepped in between them.

MAKING ROOM FOR GOD

Two final points I want to draw from this short letter. At first, they may not seem to have much to do with dealing with difficult people, but they do. Because the answer to handling those hard folks lies with you, and how you respond. And you will only be able to do that well as God gives you the wisdom, the power, and the patience.

First, did you notice the names of those helping Paul while he is being held in Rome? He references them at the end: Epaphras, Mark, Aristarchus, Demas, and Luke. He refers to these guys as "my fellow workers."

It's easy to gloss over lists of names like this when reading the Bible, but if we pause, we can find a whole unwritten backstory there. There's Mark, who is John Mark, who was given a second chance. And then there's Demas, listed as one of Paul's right-hand men. Wouldn't you have felt proud to be named among them? Paul must have seen something special in Demas to have him as part of his inner circle.

This isn't the only time he pops up in the New Testament, either. We also find him in the letter Paul writes to the Colossians, around the same time he pens his note to Philemon. In Colossians 4:14 Paul says, "Our dear friend Luke, the doctor, and Demas send greetings." So here Demas is again, this time named alongside the famous missionary doctor Luke, author of the Gospel of his name and the Book of Acts. Once more, this is heavyweight company to be part of.

But then we come to a third reference to Demas. It's in 2 Timothy, which Paul writes maybe three or four years after Philemon. And what do we find here? Paul tells Timothy, "Do your best to come to me quickly, for Demas, because he loved this world, has deserted me and has gone to Thessalonica" (4:9-10).

One of Paul's star students seems to have flamed out. He's found pursuing God to be more demanding than he likes, so he has opted for an easier life. Actually, in Greek, the name Demas means "popular." Maybe he decided that he preferred the approval of the masses to standing for the truth. Perhaps he didn't want to have to keep dealing with the difficult people that inevitably come with ministry.

Don't be a Demas! Don't let the lure of the world pull you away from God's people and God's work.

It's easy to gradually get off-track in our walk with God, if we are not careful. We may even think we are still serving Him well, for a season. In his letters to the seven churches in Revelation, Jesus tells the believers in Ephesus that He knows how they have endured great hardships for their faith. But, He goes on, "I hold this against you: You have forsaken the love you had at first" (Rev. 2:4).

How can we avoid losing our first love? The answer is the second takeaway from Paul's closing words in his letter to Philemon, "Prepare a guest room for me" (v. 22).

I hope the Bible scholars out there will give me a little leniency here to stretch the text. I know it relates to Paul's desire to visit Philemon, but I believe it also raises a question for every follower of Jesus.

Namely, is there room for Him in your life? Or have you filled that space with stuff—maybe even good stuff? Your rooms could be stacked high with clothes you are going to give away to the poor, but they have taken the place where you can host Jesus. To several of the churches in Revelation, Jesus said that He knew their deeds, but they weren't enough; He wanted their hearts.

A guest room is ready and waiting. It's not used for other things. Do you have a guest room in your heart for Jesus— time and space set aside for him to visit with you? It's there that God can meet with you. From that intimacy, you'll be prepared to go out into the world and face those difficult people.

chapter three

THE RHYTHMS AND RULES OF RELATIONSHIPS

I DIDN'T KNOW it at the time, but growing up with an unyielding taskmaster of a father prepared me a lot for life in the ministry. As I have previously mentioned, he was the first—but by no means the last—difficult person I had to learn to deal with. Through him I realized that there was an art to navigating hard relationships, but that it was possible.

Among the many other lessons he gave me was an introduction to the world of fruit. One of his several small businesses was a nursery where he bought and sold trees.

There was just about every kind of tree imaginable in that little old West Texas plot of land. We might have been the United Nations of the tree world, as far as I know. And I got to learn about them all.

Then, one day, Dad came home with what looked like a bunch of old sticks. I had to help dig deep holes for these ugly-looking pieces of wood to stand in, and it was hard work. Seemed like a real waste of time to me. Dad told me to wait and see. These were pecan and walnut trees, he said, and with the right care and cultivation, they would flourish.

Forty-some years later, wouldn't you know he was right? Those spindly, dead-seeming things have bloomed and blossomed. They provide shade for people to sit in, and maybe enjoy some of their nuts.

Through my time working Dad's nursery and my years pastoring in the heart of California's agricultural community, I have discovered that people are a lot like trees. Sometimes they may not look like much at first glance, but cultivated and cared for, they can produce wonderful fruit. Left untended, they can end up like just so much dead wood.

Healthy relationships with people are an art and a science—just like growing fruit trees. Many people who buy their fruit from the grocery think it just arrives like that by magic, but there's a whole process, a chain of events, to it getting there. You have to prepare the ground, you have to plant, you have to water and fertilize, you have to prune, you have to protect from bugs. It's the same with people. Relationships don't just happen overnight. They take time and they take work. When we forget or ignore that, we end up with problems.

What does all this have to do with difficult relationships? Two things. First, when we know how relationships are meant to grow and develop, we can prevent ourselves from coming into contact with more difficult people than we need to. As I have said, I believe that God brings difficult people into our lives for a reason, but we don't need to go looking for more than are necessary! Don't be a glutton for punishment.

Second, when we understand the way in which relationships are intended to flourish, we may be able to identify which parts of that process may have been missed or cut short with that difficult person. There just may be some great potential fruit in there.

One problem in dealing with this whole topic of relationships with difficult people is the word itself: *relationship*. For many people it implies some level of closeness or personal sharing. At the same time, its use has become too broad, too vague. The relationship you have with your spouse is very different from the relationship you have with your dentist, most likely. Some people do complain that trying to get their husband or wife to open up to them is like pulling teeth, though!

However, it is usually the case that while you have a connection with your other half, you have just interaction with your orthodontist. There is a big difference between these two "relationships."

JUDGE BY THE CONTENTS, NOT THE PACKAGING

I have learned something else from living around farmers for a long time: Some of the juiciest fruit never gets to be enjoyed because it doesn't look right. It isn't considered shapely enough for the supermarket shelves, so it gets discarded. Actually, around six billion pounds of perfectly edible fruit gets tossed each year in the United States because it doesn't "look right." It's called "cosmetic filtering."

Isn't that a commentary on our looks-obsessed, Instagram-focused world? I was encouraged to read recently about how one supermarket chain has launched a specially priced line of "imperfect but perfectly delicious" Pickuliar Picks fruits, rather than waste good produce. The fact is, wonderful fruit can come in odd-looking shapes.

The measure is not the outside but the contents. Yet that's often not the way we evaluate the people who come into our lives. We look at the externals. Ask a guy what he's looking for in a girl, and looks are probably going to be pretty high up on the list. He may talk about wanting her to be adventurous and kind to animals, too, but that may just be to make him seem deep and thoughtful!

Ask a young lady what she is looking for in a guy, and she may be less likely to focus on looks, which is good news for some! She may want someone who is intellectually stimulating or funny. I have heard that nice cologne is a big hit with women, too.

All of these things matter when you are choosing a life partner, of course. Beauty is in the eye of the beholder, as they say, so what attracts one person may not do it for another. But you need something that floats your boat if you are going to sail into the sunset with the love of your life! However, looks will fade, and after a while you will probably have heard all of his or her jokes. What makes relationships go the distance is character—what's on the inside.

We can all put on a good show for a while. When you start dating, you make sure to brush your teeth and spritz some cologne before you go out. But you can't disguise morning breath throughout many years of marriage.

This emphasis on the packaging may be heightened by social media, but it's not completely new. When Samuel the prophet went looking for Israel's next king from among Jesse's sons, he thought Eliab was the one. But God told him, "Do not consider his appearance or his height, for I have rejected him. The Lord does not look at the things people look at. People look at the outward appearance, but the Lord looks at the heart" (1 Sam. 16:7). Jesse didn't even think his youngest boy, David, was worth considering until Samuel had looked at and rejected all the other possible candidates.

Externals aren't just looks and personality. People have skills and abilities that can be attractive, too. In some cases, these may give a hint as to what's inside. If people are talented artists or musicians, you at least know that they have the patience and persistence to practice and practice. It tells you that they can be disciplined, but it doesn't tell you anything about whether they are kind to people or animals.

Then there are spiritual gifts that God gives people to extend and build up His kingdom. But let's be clear that He doesn't give these to people because they deserve them. The gift doesn't say anything about the recipient, but the way they shepherd and use it can speak volumes.

Just because someone operates with a great spiritual gift, it does not necessarily mean hr or she is a great spiritual person. I've known people in ministry who I would welcome to the platform as a visitor because I know they have a powerful gift, but I wouldn't want them staying around long-term because I know they don't have a lot of character.

A gift tells you about the giver, not the recipient. If I buy a diamond for my wife and I hand it to her, it does not say one thing about how much she loves me. It says everything about how much I love her. We need to be careful not to let gifts fool us.

WHAT GIFTS DON'T TELL US ABOUT SOMEONE

Sometimes our giftings can get in the way of our development. We start to believe our own press releases, if you will, and we begin to think we really are a bit of all that. This is why we need to develop good relationships with people who will lovingly hold us to account.

As the late Ed Cole, author of the bestselling book *Maximized Manhood*, so rightly said, a man's gift will take him to a level that his character can't support. He was speaking specifically to men, but the same is true for women, of course.

Not long after I became a Christian, I got to know a guy who was a really gifted musician. He could touch your spirit in song like nobody else I knew. One day, I was riding with him in his car when his little poodle dog sitting in the back got sick. The poor animal threw up all over the rear of the vehicle. My friend pulled his car over to the side the road, jumped out and grabbed that hound and almost spanked the life out of it. I was shocked; the guy's anger was so out of control I almost feared he might start on me next. He may have been a sweet singer but he was a mean stinger too.

Jesus warned about people who seemed to be one thing but were another. "Watch out for false prophets," He said. They would come in sheep's clothing, but they would really be wolves, He went on. How to spot them? He gave the answer in Matthew 7:16-20:

By their fruit you will recognize them. Do people pick grapes from thornbushes, or figs from thistles? Likewise, every good tree bears good fruit, but a bad tree bears bad fruit. A good tree cannot bear bad fruit, and a bad tree cannot bear good fruit. Every tree that does not bear good fruit is cut down and thrown into the fire. Thus, by their fruit you will recognize them.

There is more to buying good fruit at the store than picking the ones that look good. There are all sorts of buyer's guides and charts available online, explaining what to look for in terms of color and firmness. Paul gave us a guide for evaluating people in his letter to the Galatians. The acts of the flesh are obvious, he said (5:19-21):

… sexual immorality, impurity and debauchery; idolatry and witchcraft; hatred, discord, jealousy, fits of rage, selfish ambition, dissensions, factions and envy; drunkenness, orgies, and the like. I warn you, as I did before, that those who live like this will not inherit the kingdom of God.

The fruit of the Holy Spirit within us, evidence of our relationship with God, meanwhile, is (5:22-24):

… love, joy, peace, forbearance, kindness, goodness, faithfulness, gentleness and self-control. Against such things there is no law. Those who belong to Christ Jesus have crucified the flesh with its passions and desires.

Notice that Jesus warned against false prophets. Not false tax collectors or false centurions. He didn't tell His followers to be on guard against people in the everyday world but people in the religious world.

Just because people turn up in church with their hair brushed right, clean clothes, and big smiles and they can quote the Bible doesn't mean we accept everything they say as gospel. I'm not talking about being suspicious of everyone, just appropriately cautious. I don't know anything about that newcomer: whether they pay their bills on time, if they treat their spouse kindly, or how well they tip their server at the restaurant. All that only becomes evident over time.

TWO KEYS IN RELATIONSHIPS

You can only really love at the level you know. Let's imagine a reunion at the airport. John is in the military and he's been gone for many months serving our country. He comes back and there's his family waiting to greet him with balloons and big smiles. John snatches up his little baby because he is so glad to see him, but the child is a little cautious because he doesn't really know his daddy because he has been gone so long. The little guy starts looking around for his momma. John takes his sweet wife in his arms and there's kissing and hugging like it's the end of the world. That's a whole other level of love. But don't miss who's standing at the rear, waiting for her moment: John's mother. The woman who brought him into the world and who loves him in the way only a mom can. That's a different level of love, too.

Developing relationships takes time. One of the problems of our techy, appy world is that we think everything can be done instantly. Even before online dating apps there was speed dating, started by a young Jewish man looking to provide an environment in which Jewish singles could meet. Two people get to sit down together and chat for eight minutes or so before moving on to someone else. At the end of the evening, they identify which of the folks they met they had any interest in, and if that is reciprocated the two parties are put in touch to take things farther.

Today there are more than one hundred speed-dating businesses in the world, and the concept has been the subject of study by researchers at the University of Pennsylvania. They surveyed more than ten thousand speed daters and found something really interesting.[6] Most participants

6. Clark, Josh. "How Speed Dating Works." *Howstuffworks.com.* https://people.howstuffworks.com/speed-dating4.htm. Retrieved February 7, 2020.

made a decision on whether or not they had any interest in the other person within the first three seconds. Talk about first impressions. Even more significantly, most of them made that judgment on a sense or a feeling that often overrode the preferences they had expressed in filling out their pre-date information and interests. The researchers concluded that "in the context of a speed date, the usual rules of attraction go out the window."

Appearances can be deceptive. A friend of mine went to a Christian speed-dating event one time and found himself sitting across from a sweet-looking young lady. Using one of the conversation-starter prompts on the table, he asked her, "So what's your favorite movie of all time?"

She looked at him brightly. "*The Silence of the Lambs*," she told him.

This was not what he had been expecting, as you might imagine. His mind was more along the lines maybe of *Little Women* or *It's a Wonderful Life*. Something sweet and wholesome.

Now, I'm not saying that choice makes her a bad person, but an R-rated movie about a serial killer who skins and eats his female victims is certainly an unusual one. I for sure don't remember ever having heard of a Bible study based on it.

Dating apps now make in-person speed dating seem positively slow in comparison. People look at a photo and read a brief bio and "swipe right" in seconds. The pace at which choices are made accelerate everything else. So, Darren and Lynn connect on their smartphones and agree to meet up at Starbucks. They have a nice visit for an hour or so, at the end of which they exchange actual phone numbers. Darren thinks maybe he will text her and see about meeting up again sometime soon. Later that night, his phone pings and there's a message from Lynn—with a nude photo of herself. They have gone from getting to know you to sexting in a matter of hours.

I'm not being a fuddy-duddy. I'm all for nudity—in the right time and place. And so is God! Nudity is not a bad thing to Him. Remember that Adam went to sleep one day, woke up scratching his side, and looked over to see naked Eve. His response was where we get the word woman: "Woah, man!" And God didn't tell Adam and Eve, …"No"; He told them, "Enjoy!" But in the context of a relationship that God had blessed.

Rushing ahead ends in heartache. Such an undiscerning approach to relationships violates two important concepts when it comes to interacting with other people: expectations and information.

EXPECTATIONS: When reality does not meet expectation, the result is disappointment. Proper expectations will ward off disappointment every time, because you aren't looking for more than is reasonable. It's like building a house on the sand: Without a firm foundation, that place isn't going to survive a storm.

Jesus spoke about this, of course, but you may not have noticed the context in which He did so. His warning comes in Matthew 7:24-26, right after He cautioned listeners to be careful to distinguish between true and false prophets and true and false disciples. He followed that alert by saying, "Therefore everyone who hears these words of mine and puts them into practice is like a wise man who built his house on the rock" (v. 24). His application had relationships specifically in mind.

Think about some of the relationships in your life, especially those with difficult people. Are you trying to build too tall a structure on too shallow a foundation? You need to go low before you can go high.

INFORMATION: One of the big measures of a relationship is the kind of information that you share. When I was growing up, people didn't go round spilling their guts to others the first time they met them. That seems to be changing a bit. People can be surprisingly open on social media about what's going on in their lives; I know lots about people I have never even met in person. Of course, often we only give people a carefully edited version of our lives, but we are generally still more widely "known" than in the past.

It should be that the deeper you go in a relationship, the deeper the exchange of information. We see this in Jesus' life. When He spoke to His disciples at the Last Supper, He told them, "I no longer call you servants, because a servant does not know his master's business. Instead, I have called you friends, for everything that I learned from my Father I have made known to you" (John 15:15). The point is that their relationship developed and changed as He revealed more to them.

Jesus spoke to the crowds in parables, but He explained the parables to His disciples. He didn't treat all twelve of them the same, however. Peter and the brothers James and John were His inner circle. He took them up the mountain when He was transfigured. They got to witness His encounter with Moses and Elijah, when God the Father spoke from heaven, "This is my Son, whom I love. Listen to Him!" On the way down from the mountain, Jesus "gave them orders not to tell anyone what they had seen until the Son of Man had risen from the dead" (Mark 9:9). At the Last Supper, Jesus weighed what to tell His disciples. "I have much more to say to you," He said, "more than you can now bear" (John 16:12).

We need to be wise about the information we share. Are those people qualified to handle what you have, just yet? Do you know their character well enough? Be cautious about dumping on someone about how bad your divorce was the first time you meet them. It might feel good in the moment, but it may not be helpful in the long run.

Leaders in particular need wisdom in knowing what to tell who and when. I've heard it said that there is a difference between authenticity and transparency, and that's really true. We should be authentic—real—in who we are, but that doesn't mean everyone needs to know everything all the time. When I was a young pastor, I made a poor judgment call one time. I watched a movie that had some questionable content in it. I knew that I should have switched it off, but I kept watching all the way through to the end. I felt so miserable afterward; I knew I had done wrong. I told God how sorry I was and prayed for forgiveness.

I decided that I needed to repent before the whole congregation. Before the service, I told my prayer buddy, a wise older guy, about what I intended to do, and asked him to pray for me.

He laid a hand on my arm. "Mike, let's not do that today," he said gently. "You've confessed your sins to God, and He has forgiven you. Let's not take the whole congregation down a road it has no need to be going down."

Thankfully, I heeded his advice. Keeping quiet was not being deceitful, it was being wise. It was recognizing what people could bear, as Jesus had done. I'd shared my wrongdoing with my friend, and I had confessed to God, and there was no need to involve everyone else. Doing so would only have left me publicly humiliated and undermined my leadership. It's not that I had to pretend to be better than I was; in fact, I have since shared that story with people individually when I felt it was appropriate. Some things are just on a "need to know" basis.

To this day, I do not share all my faults with just anybody. I do have some close pastor friends I can and do call up, though, and say, "You know what? You know everything about me. I just need you to stop everything right now and I need you to throw down in the Spirit right now. We need to pray." God moves in moments like that. James 5:16 says that Christians should "confess your sins to each other and pray for each other so that you may be healed."

CALLING OUT THE BEST IN YOU

Although I've said that God sends difficult people into our lives to refine and improve us, it doesn't mean we need to be on our guard all the time. There is certainly some wisdom in pacing the development and growth of any new relationship, but I'm not suggesting that whenever someone new comes into your orbit your first reaction should be, "Uh-oh, here comes potential trouble!"

The exact opposite could be true, in fact. God could be sending someone to keep you out of trouble with difficult people.

There's a great example of this in David's life. For the most part, he handled his difficult relationship with Saul well. He didn't get resentful and angry. He continued to honor Saul in the face of great hardship. He chose not to take things into his own hands when he had the chance. But maybe all that took its toll and things started to come out sideways.

It's not uncommon. When we know we are facing a test, we can knuckle down and step up to it. But that may take so much out of us that we end up having less patience and kindness for the people on the fringes of our lives. You can cope with that domineering, demanding boss at work all day, but you lose it with the old lady driver who cuts in front of you on the commute home. You put up with that ornery old relative at Thanksgiving dinner, but snap at the kids when everyone has gone home. If we are not careful, difficult people can cause us to treat other people less well.

That may have been what happened with David. The story is to be found in 1 Samuel 25. David was hiding out in the desert of Paran, having refused to take the opportunity to kill Saul when he slipped into a cave to relieve himself not knowing that David and his men were hiding out there.

"The Lord forbid that I should do such a thing to my master, the Lord's anointed, or lay my hand on him; for he is the anointed of the Lord," David said (v. 6).

One day David sent some of his guys out to Nabal, a wealthy landowner, to ask for some supplies. They'd never taken anything from Nabal, nor mistreated any of his people, they pointed out: How about a little helping hand?

Nabal is described as "surly and mean in his dealings" (v. 3), and we see that in his response. He said to his visitors (vs. 10-11):

Who is this David? Who is this son of Jesse? Many servants are breaking away from their masters these days. Why should I take my bread and water, and the meat I have slaughtered for my shearers, and give it to men coming from who knows where?

When David heard about this response, he just about blew a gasket. He hadn't been asking for the world, just a few groceries in return for keeping things peaceful, and this was the thanks he got? David went from zero to 100 mph in seconds. The man who in just the previous chapter had refused to pick up a sword against Saul, who had tried to kill him, now snatched it up and told his men to grab theirs because Nabal had been selfish. Talk about a lack of perspective.

With steam coming out of his ears, David led four hundred of his small army to go and teach Nabal a lesson. Heads were going to roll!

Fortunately for Nabal—and David—one of his servants overheard the way Nabal had snubbed his visitors and went to tell Nabal's wife, Abigail. She quickly rounded up a few grocery carts full of supplies, loaded them onto donkeys, and headed off to intercept David.

Falling prostrate before him, she begged him to think twice. Abigail showed how humility can win us someone's ear when confrontation may not. She was able to diffuse the situation:

Please pay no attention, my lord, to that wicked man Nabal. He is just like his name—his name means Fool, and folly goes with him... as the LORD your God lives and as you live, since the LORD has kept you from bloodshed and from avenging yourself with your own hands, may your enemies and all who are intent on harming my lord be like Nabal... you fight the LORD's battles, and no wrongdoing will be found in you as long as you live... When the LORD has fulfilled for my lord every good thing he promised concerning him and has appointed him ruler over Israel, my lord will not have on his conscience the staggering burden of needless bloodshed or of having avenged himself (1 Sam. 25:24-31).

Abigail's desperate intervention worked. It stopped David in his tracks long enough for the red mist to evaporate and for him to see clearly. How might God's purposes for David have been set back had she not been successful, I wonder? Through her words and her actions, Abigail helped avert what could have become a serious roadblock on David's journey to the throne.

Notice that she referred to David becoming the ruler of Israel; she reminded him of his destiny. She spoke to his highest version. Nabal brought out the fighter in David; Abigail brought out the king in him. Nabal provoked a re-actionary spirit; Abigail promoted a royalty attitude. We all need people like that in our lives—and there may be times when we need to be willing to risk stepping out in front of others to do the same for them, to remind them of their destinies.

David recognized Abigail as a gift from God. "Praise be to the Lord, the God of Israel, who has sent you to-day to meet me," he told her (v. 32). When you are all too ready to rumble over something a difficult person has done, be open to an Abigail coming to keep you from doing what you will come to regret. And keep in mind that you may get to be an Abigail to someone else's mad-as-hell David. Don't settle for being an avenger when you are called to be royalty.

It's also worth noting that while David chose not to lift a hand against Nabal, God did. A week or so later, "the Lord struck Nabal, and he died" (v. 38). I wonder whether Paul had this in mind when he wrote to the church in Rome. He certainly had some wise words for dealing with difficult people: "Bless those who persecute you. Bless and do not curse… Do not repay anyone evil for evil…. If it is possible on your part, live at peace with everyone" (Rom. 12:14-18). Then he added, "Do not avenge yourselves, beloved, but leave room for God's wrath. For it is written: 'Vengeance is Mine; I will repay, says the Lord'" (v. 19).

Don't take things into your own hands when facing difficult people. Leave them in God's.

chapter four

IT'S TIME TO LET THEM GO

W HEN KAREN AND I moved houses recently, I came across an old photograph I hadn't seen in ages. It was a group shot of a bunch of church people we'd been close with many years ago. Looking at the picture made me realize how much times have changed. Not just because of the out-dated fashions, but because of how some of the lives there have gone.

Some people spun out in their faith, for one reason or another. Others fell out of sorts with each other. It's a fact of life: Anyone who has been married for any length of time knows that the honeymoon doesn't last forever. At some point, you realize that your spouse isn't quite as perfect as you thought they were. And coming to that awareness brings about a second really important discovery—that you're not quite as perfect as you thought you were, either. After all, if you were, their imperfections wouldn't bug you so much, right?

The same is true for other close friendships. Fact is, even the strongest and richest of relationships is going to be tested over time, because we all make mistakes and let people down. Sometimes we do it accidentally, and sometimes we do it intentionally. Sometimes we expect more of people than is reasonable. Either way, at some stage we are going to be left with a gap between what we hoped for and what is. And something is going to fill this space.

Real relationships face testing because they are constantly growing and changing. I am not the same guy I was when I married Karen. She has changed through the years, too. Like all long-married couples, we have had to learn and adapt to the new person. The same is true with long-time friends.

When I started out in ministry, I was way more conservative than I am these days. Not in terms of what I believe about the gospel, and people's need for a Savior. More in terms of what that might look like in everyday life. Having become a Christian through the old holiness movement, I was very big into doing the right thing. I still believe that how we live is important, but I also have come to the conclusion that we need to be careful about making judgments based on external appearances alone. It's about the fruits rather than the "fronts" that people project. That's what matters.

One time I got to talk with an elderly man who had been an influential leader in the holiness movement during the 1940s. I asked him what he thought about the difference between now and then, between the days when we preached more fire and brimstone and when we're more focused on being seeker-sensitive.

"Well, back in my day, we got less people into heaven, but they were more cleaned-up and better looking," he told me. "These days, it seems like folks aren't as concerned about sanctification and holiness as we were. They are about getting more people into heaven in less shape. I think I prefer the latter."

CATS DON'T BARK

Adjusting our expectations, as I discussed in the previous chapter, is key to reducing unnecessary conflict. I'm not talking about settling for less, but if we have a more realistic idea of how things might be, we are less likely to end up getting let down. Proper expectations will save you from a lot of heartache.

If you understand the nature of something, its behavior will never surprise you. By way of example, I never expect a dog to meow. Nor do I wait for a cat to bark. Why not? Because that's not who they are or what they do. Dogs don't meow, and cats don't bark; that's just the way it is. Wave a cape in front of a bull, and it will charge at it. That's what bulls do. Matadors don't get upset about that—they just make sure they hold the cape in such a way that the bull doesn't get them. That's worth remembering when you are dealing with difficult people: You may not be able to stop them charging, but you don't have to stand right in their path!

Let's maneuver this away from the animal kingdom. With a few exceptions, don't expect teenagers to look at the world the way you do as an adult. Their brains haven't finished developing, and their bodies are going through all sorts of crazy changes, so why would you think they are going to act like grownups? It's naive at best. And what about the differences between men and women—which are vast, whatever the people who want to blur the idea of there being two distinct genders want you to believe.

In a nutshell, men are like a light switch on the wall. On. Off. Not too complicated. Women, meanwhile, are like the cockpit control plane of a jumbo jet: an array of gauges and dials and switches that work in concert. I'm over simplifying, of course, but the point remains: When you better understand who and what you are dealing with, the less likely you are to end up being disappointed.

However, there will come a time, even with your best efforts, when you are left wondering about someone in your life. Jesus Himself said so. We like to quote Him declaring that "with God all things are possible" (Matt. 19:26), and that is the core message of the gospel: Though you may be dead in your sins, Jesus can bring you to new life! He not only preached the impossible, He demonstrated it— He made blind eyes see, He made deaf ears hear, He made crippled legs dance. He even brought the dead back to life. Jesus was big on unlikely things being possible. With Him, miracles could always happen.

And yet He also knew human nature. He knew that not all relationships would be trouble-free. And that awareness led Him to add a qualifier to His all-things-are-possible message. Just one time, He told them that not all things were possible. In Luke 17:1, He said, "It is *impossible* that no offenses should come" (NKJV, emphasis added).

That's quite an emphatic statement, but He was speaking from personal experience.

EVEN CLOSE RELATIONSHIPS CHANGE

If ever two people should have had a problem-free relationship, surely it was John the Baptist and his cousin Jesus. Their bond even pre-dated their birth. When Mary discovered she had been chosen to bear Jesus, she went to her cousin, Elizabeth, who was pregnant with John. Luke 1:41 tells us, "When Elizabeth heard Mary's greeting, the baby [John] leaped in her womb, and Elizabeth was filled with the Holy Spirit."

Both babies' births had been foretold in Old Testament prophecies. John's arrival wasn't quite as miraculous as that of Jesus, but it required God's hand. Zechariah the priest and his wife, Elizabeth, were advanced in years and childless when an angel of the Lord appeared to him to declare they would conceive. And this would be no ordinary child. The angel said:

He will be a joy and delight to you, and many will rejoice because of his birth, for he will be great in the sight of the

*Lord. He is never to take wine or other fermented drink,
and he will be filled with the Holy Spirit even before he
is born. He will bring back many of the people of Israel
to the Lord their God. And he will go on before the Lord,
in the spirit and power of Elijah, to turn the hearts of the
parents to their children and the disobedient to the wisdom of the righteous—to make ready a people prepared
for the Lord (Luke 1:14-17).*

We don't know much about their younger years, but
it's not unreasonable to believe that John and Jesus may
have known each other as they were growing up, and even
hung out some. Extended families were common in those
days. And their parents seem to have been close; after all,
Mary chose to go to Elizabeth when she learned of her
incredible news.

By the time he was about 28 or so years of age, John was
at the top of his preaching game. He had stepped into the
destiny spoken over him in Isaiah 40:3-5:

*A voice of one calling:
"In the wilderness prepare
the way for the Lord;
make straight in the desert*

a highway for our God.
Every valley shall be raised up,

every mountain and hill made low;
the rough ground shall become level,
the rugged places a plain.
And the glory of the Lord
For the mouth of the Lord has spoken."

John was sort of awkward, if not downright difficult. He certainly didn't seem to have heard about the seeker-sensitive movement. He dressed weird and he ate funny: an outfit of camel's hair held together with a leather belt, and a diet of wild locusts and honey. He was a bit of an oddball, but he had an anointing. People flocked to hear him. They weren't drawn by the great venue: He preached out in the hot, dry wilderness. Nor were they attracted by his smooth talking and great jokes.

He let them have it with both barrels, preaching repentance with a capital R. His message was right to the point, "Man, if you guys don't get right with God, you're going to hell in a hand basket." When they told him they had repented, he didn't just say okay. He pressed them, "All right then, bring me fruit that proves to me that you have repented. I hear all you Pharisees and all you religious people talking a good game, but I don't see any real evidence."

No two ways about it, John was one rough-around-the-edges guy. But he was so anointed that even tax collectors and attorneys were getting saved. That's some serious salvation. And then, one day, it all turned.

John had gotten to be part of an amazing moment, seeing heaven open up and the Holy Spirit descend on Jesus in the form of a dove. But John had just been the opening act: *Now please welcome to the stage, Jesus of Nazareth!* And John was fine with that. "There he is," he told the crowds. "That's the One. That's the Messiah. He's the One all the prophets have been speaking about. He must increase. I must decrease now."

As Jesus' star began to rise, John's started to fade, but he kept to his message of repentance. It got him into trouble with Herod, the ruler of Galilee. John rebuked Herod for taking his sister-in-law as his wife and ended up getting thrown in jail as a result.

Sitting under lock and key, knowing that his life was in danger, he began to wonder. He sent two of his followers out to where Jesus was now holding meetings. He wanted them to ask his cousin a question:

Are you the one who is to come, or should we expect someone else? (Matt. 11:3).

It's important not to misunderstand what John was asking. He wasn't really checking to see if Jesus was the Son of God. John wasn't doubting his own revelation and experience. He knew who Jesus was. He was saying, "Hey, Jesus, have you forgotten me?" "Hey, Jesus, are you coming to see me or to get me out?" "Hey, Jesus, help!"

When John's messengers found Jesus, He was busy. He had been healing people of their sicknesses and preaching about the kingdom of God. He told John's guys:

Go and tell John the things which you hear and see: The blind see and the lame walk; the lepers are cleansed and the deaf hear; the dead are raised up and the poor have the gospel preached to them. And blessed is he who is not offended because of Me (Matthew 11:4-6 [NKJV]).

THE DEADLY DANGER OF TAKING OFFENSE

Jesus' response to John's inquiry is really interesting. He doesn't seem to be particularly sympathetic to John's plight. No "Hang in there, Cuz," or "Hope I can get to see you soon," or "I'll see what I can do for you."

Rather, He starts by reminding John that what's happening is what he, John, had been preaching about and preparing the way for. And then Jesus tells him not to be offended.

He is telling John that times have changed, things are different now. It's like a young couple having a baby and doting on it, and then along comes number two and their attention is divided. Now, parents will often tell you that they think they can never find more love than they've had for their firstborn, but when others do come along, the love just somehow multiplies, and there is still more than enough to go around.

That may be the case, but it sure isn't how it feels to baby number one. He or she has had all the attention and suddenly is having to share it with someone else?

It's one of the many important but painful and necessary lessons you learn growing up in a family: The world does not revolve around you. If you can have this one solidly under your belt by the time you are twenty, it will save you a lot of heartache.

John the Baptist knew this truth well: He'd even told people that he needed to fade away as Jesus gained popularity. But when push came to shove, John found it hard to accept.

Maybe it was more difficult for him because he'd been an only child himself!

Whatever the case, Jesus warned him against taking offense. He didn't address the offense itself. Actually, I don't think that Jesus cares too much if we get offended, for a couple of reasons. First, the offense is an opportunity for us to grow in love and grace and forgiveness. And second, He knows that sometimes we need to be offended. In fact, our salvation depends upon it.

1 Peter 2:8 describes Jesus as "A stone that causes people to stumble and a rock that makes them fall." He would rather you be offended on this side of death than end up going to hell and being offended for eternity.

Yet offenses are one of the biggest causes of church problems. People let each other down somehow or misunderstand each other, they get their feelings hurt, and they let that fester. Untreated wounds are a source of potential infection.

Unity in the church is so important to God's purposes! "How good and pleasant it is when God's people live together in unity!" says Psalm 133:1. It's like the oil with which the Old Testament priests were anointed, where "the Lord bestows His blessing, even life forevermore" (v. 3).

That is why the devil is always on the lookout for people who are carrying an offense. He wants to get his hooks into them. In his book about it, John Bevere calls taking an offense *The Bait of Satan*. The Greek word for offense is *skandalon*, meaning bait or stumbling stone—something that will ensnare you or trip you up.

The real problem here is not what someone may have said or done to you; it's how you choose to respond. Will you let that difficult person cause something to lodge in you, like a splinter? If you do, the issue switches from what may have been their sin to yours, in the way that you respond. You aren't responsible for what they do about their sin, but you are certainly responsible for what you do about yours. And if we are honest, hurt is often to do with pride. Remember that the middle letter of both sin and pride is *I*. Pride won't solve anything; in fact, Proverbs 13:10 says that from it "comes nothing but strife" (NKJV).

Holding on to offenses and refusing to forgive doesn't just lead to spiritual problems. It can also be a factor in physical ill-health. According to one study, more than 60 percent of cancer patients admitted to having unforgiveness issues.[7]

7. Johnson, Lorie. "The Deadly Consequences of Unforgiveness." *CBN News*. https://www1.cbn.com/cbnnews/healthscience/2015/june/the-deadly-consequences-of-unforgiveness. June 22, 2015.

Another found that carrying anger into old age is associated with higher levels of inflammation and chronic illness.[8] It dampens and shuts down your immune system, so you are less able to fight off sickness. And it can lead to depression.

So why do we hold onto hurts when they are so bad for us? Because, like the character played by actress Reese Witherspoon in the HBO series, *Big Little Lies*, said, "I love my grudges. I tend to them like litte pets."

Having become aware of the health dangers of unforgiveness, Dr. Frederic Luskin founded the Stanford Forgiveness Project to help people learn how to let go of old hurts. First, he says, slow down. Go for a walk. Take in a deep breath. "You have to counter-condition the stress response when it happens," he says.[9]

Next, you have to refocus, change your story "from that of a victim to a more heroic" one. For believers, that means you need to quit talking about how someone has done you wrong and start talking about how good God is, and

---

8. Ibid.

9. Herrera, Tim. "Let Go of Your Grudges. They're Doing You No Good." *The New York Times.* https://www.nytimes.com/2019/05/19/smarter-living/let-go-of-your-grudges-theyre-doing-you-no-good.html May 19, 2019.

how good He has always been to you. When you focus on Scripture, you are not focused on grudges.

Dr. Luskin's final tip: Remind yourself of the one simple truth that life doesn't always turn out the way you want it to. "Forgiveness is a learnable skill," he says. "It just takes a little time."

Those are all good ideas, but they are treatment rather than prevention. Let me suggest a way to avoid getting infected with resentment in the first place: Read your Bible. Yes, it's really that simple. Psalm 119:165 (KJV) says, "Great peace have they which love thy law: and nothing shall offend them."

When people come to me all bent out of shape about some little thing or another, many times I will ask them how much they have been reading their Bible lately. I have found over the years that there seems to be a correlation between the amount of time someone spends in the Bible and that person's capacity for being easily ticked off by something or someone. I believe that's because the more we allow God's Word to sink into our hearts, the less room there will be for offenses. So maybe you need to get your face out of Facebook and get your face into His Book for a while!

You may also want to think about getting baptized, if you haven't. *What*, I hear you say? *What does baptism have to do with offenses and hurts and unforgiveness?* Well, if pride is the splinter that can get lodged in our hearts and turn nasty, then humility is the ointment.

There is an interesting aside in the account of John sending messengers to ask if Jesus is the one he should be expecting. It's in Luke 7:29-30:

> *(All the people, even the tax collectors, when they heard Jesus' words, acknowledged that God's way was right, because they had been baptized by John. But the Pharisees and the experts in the law rejected God's purpose for themselves, because they had not been baptized by John.)*

It's easy to miss at first glance, but there is something significant here. All those that received Jesus' message had been baptized. Those who did not receive His message had not been baptized. And who were they? The Pharisees and experts in the law, who thought that they knew more about God and His ways than John the Baptist!

Before Jesus ascended into heaven, He gave His disciples their marching orders. He told them to go into all the world, preach the good news, and baptize people in the name of the Father, the Son, and the Holy Spirit. Now, I know that baptism is a symbol of our spiritual rebirth, but I don't know all the reasons why Jesus insisted on it. In the same way, I know that taking communion is significant, but I can't explain all the reasons why. I just know that as Jesus' followers, we are supposed to be baptized and take communion. You might be surprised by how many people don't follow these simple instructions.

I was talking recently with a young lady about her faith walk. I asked whether or not she had been baptized in water, and she said she had not because she didn't want to get her hair wet in front of other people. Her appearance mattered more to her than being obedient to God's Word.

A visiting evangelist with a gift of healing came to our church one time and was praying for people. An elderly woman with hearing problems came up, and he prayed for her. When he asked if she could hear any better she said she could not. It was kind of awkward.

"We have a problem here," the preacher said. "Everyone else I have prayed for has been healed." He asked the woman if she had ever been baptized in water? Again, she had not.

"Well, go and be baptized and come back, and you'll be healed," he said.

The woman left and never did follow through. Maybe she felt that after years of serving God, she just didn't need to be baptized.

The real point here is not baptism or communion or some other area that God may be speaking to you about. It's about obedience, which requires humility. There is just something about water baptism, for example, that breaks something off you in the area of pride. You stand there in front of a bunch of people and humble yourself. You admit you have been a sinner and need God's grace and forgiveness. Pride gets drowned by humility.

LETTING IT GO

If you're carrying an offense against someone, you have to deal with it. In the words of that famous ear-candy song from the kids' movie, *Frozen*, "Let it Go!" I learned this lesson early in my Christian life. I'd been saved just six months or so when I went to hear a well-known preacher who was holding a crusade at the Coliseum in Lubbock, Texas. My conversion had been powerful; I'd gone from being a waster to being on-fire for God, telling everyone about Jesus. I was keen to soak up everything I could about the Lord, so I was glad to get a seat on the front row.

I'd just received my refund check from the IRS that day—$276. That was a good chunk of change back in the seventies. I'd tucked a twenty-dollar bill inside my wallet to give to the offering, and planned to put the rest in savings. However, when the offering bucket started to pass along the row, I felt convicted. I reached into my wallet, pulled out all the money that was there—all my IRS refund—and dropped it into the bucket.

That was when the speaker, up on the platform, shouted out. "Stop the offering, stop the offering!" Then he looked down at me. "You haven't given anything to the Lord tonight!" he thundered.

I was shocked. I was hurt. And I was ticked. I might have had a life-changing encounter with the Holy Spirit, but I was still a young guy with lots of rough edges. I could feel my indignation rising: I'd just emptied my wallet, and I was being singled out in front of everybody as a cheapwad. Then I felt God speak to me. *Just let it go*, He said, *don't be offended*. So I sat still, and simply passed the bucket on to the person next to me.

I wasn't aware of it at the time, but making that choice proved to be really important. In the years that followed, God gave me a gift for raising money for His kingdom work. I have been blessed to raise millions of dollars in donations, both for projects in churches I was leading and for others. I believe that grace was given to me because I chose not to be offended in the area of how I handle money.

Fast-forward about thirty years, and I was in a restaurant with a new pastor on our staff when I saw that same preacher sitting at a nearby table with his entourage. He had become even more famous in the intervening years. Seeing him took me back to that evening long ago when I had been unfairly shamed. I went over to greet him. It could have been tempting to tell him the story and explain what really happened, but I chose not to.

Instead, I introduced myself, and told him how much I appreciated his ministry. I said that I wanted to pay the bill for him and his team. I took it, said it had been a pleasure to meet him, and left without saying anything else. I felt like God had orchestrated that encounter to let me know that the man's long-ago rebuke hadn't gotten to me.

The new staff gal that my wife and I had been eating with asked me about it all as we left, and I told her the backstory. I told her how God has used me to raise money for His work, and how I believe that the devil wanted to snuff that gift out before it really got released, by getting me to hold onto an offense.

It's a common strategy of the enemy. He wants the weeds of woundedness to strangle the fruits of the Spirit. That's why in Hebrews 12:15 we are warned to be careful that no "bitter root grows up to cause trouble and defile many." Notice that it doesn't just affect the individual. Like a virus, it spreads to others.

To be honest, until I saw the preacher in the restaurant, I'd forgotten about the offering incident. Not by accident, but by design—I chose not to remember. That's consistent with the way God treats us. He promised, "For I will forgive their wickedness and will remember their sins no more" (Jer. 31:34).

Some people believe there are situations and hurts that it's just not possible to put behind us, but that's not true. One time I asked a retiring denominational superintendent how he slept at night after years and years of seeing the ugly side of church life, with all its disappointments, up close. "I've forgotten most of it," he told me with a smile. I think too of Joseph, who named his firstborn Manasseh—which means "causing to forget"—"because God has made me forget all my trouble and all my father's household" (Gen. 41:51).

Hurt feelings can linger, though. When that happens, we may need to take some steps, some action, to loosen our emotional grip. If an offense is eating at you, you may have to go to the person. The longer you wait to go have that conversation, the bigger it grows.

When I was in seminary, this old preacher came to speak in the chapel, and he told a story that I have never forgotten. He had been pastoring out in this country church, where one of the members was a Mr. Wellingham, a farmer who had a beloved dog that went everywhere with him.

One day Mr. Wellingham came home to discover that his sweet dog had been shot and killed. Gruesomely, its head had been chopped off and placed on a fence post as a kind of warning. He knew immediately what had happened: The old codger across the street had shot his dog for getting in the man's chicken coop.

Mr. Wellingham was furious. He had one thought on his mind; he was going into the house to get his gun, and he was going to shoot the neighbor's prize bull over in the pasture. He went to his gun rack, loaded his rifle, and started to head out the door when his wife asked what he was doing.

"You saw our dead dog," Mr. Wellingham replied. "You know he did it for our dog's getting in that chicken coop. I am sick of that neighbor. I am going to go shoot his bull."

His wife put herself between him and the door. "You can't do that," she told him.

"Yes, I can. Get out of my way, woman."

"No, you can't do that. You have got to forgive that man."

"That man killed the best dog I ever had."

"Forgive him."

It took her a while, but she finally talked him off the ledge. Mr. Wellingham sat down and cooled off. Finally he said, "Well, what do you want me to do?"

She told him that he needed to bake his neighbor a cake.

Mr. Wellingham thought that was just about the dumbest thing he had ever heard, and he told his wife so. She just sat there and talked to him about it some more. Eventually, Mr. Wellingham gave in and told his wife, okay, she could bake a cake for their neighbor.

"I've already got it made," she told him.

She went and got the cake, put it in her husband's hands, and guided him out through the door—without his rifle. Mr. Wellingham couldn't believe he was walking across the street with a home-baked cake in his hands. As he neared his neighbor's house he could see the man looking out through the window, with a rifle in his hand.

Somehow, Mr. Wellingham forced himself to go and knock on the door. It opened.

"What do you want, Wellingham?"

Mr. Wellingham took a deep breath. "I know what happened today," he said. "My dog probably got in your chicken coop again, and you probably shot him. I am pretty sure that's what happened. But I just wanted to let you know that I'm a Christian, and I forgive you. My wife has baked you a cake. Enjoy."

The neighbor could not believe his ears. He invited Mr. Wellingham in, leaned his gun up against the wall, and asked his neighbor to sit down. Then he went over to the cupboard and pulled out two plates. He cut a slice of that fresh cake, passed it over and said, "You take the first bite, Wellingham." Maybe he was worried it had been poisoned.

Mr. Wellingham started eating that cake and the neighbor began to cry. "I don't understand. I don't understand," he said. "I shot your dog. I knew you were going to shoot my bull. And when you did, I was going to shoot you. I was ready. I knew how this was all going to play out, but you have totally messed this whole thing up.

"What makes you think like this, Wellingham?"

"Jesus forgave us of so much," Mr. Wellingham told him. "He calls us to forgive as he forgave." That day, Mr. Wellingham's wife became his Abigail, as I talked about in the previous chapter. As a result, he led his neighbor to faith in the Lord Jesus Christ. The difficult old codger ended up becoming a deacon in the church.

If you are a dog lover, you know that's tough love! But it is what we are called to do, as followers of Jesus. Instead of serving a slice of cold revenge to a difficult person, we should offer a slice of fresh cake instead. Refuse to take the bait, and offer a gift in its place.

chapter five

THE WOUND OF BETRAYAL

SOME OF THE most difficult people we will ever need to deal with are those who have at one time been dearest to us. It's one thing to have to face that cranky co-worker or nasty neighbor. It's a whole other level of hard to handle those to whom we have given something of our heart, only to be betrayed.

There's probably no greater pain than when one spouse decides they want out of their marriage, especially when there has been unfaithfulness on their part. It's the ultimate rejection. But other betrayals can run deep too—in extended family relationships, in business ventures, in church ministry. You're left feeling disappointed, exposed, shamed, used, wronged.

It's not surprising, then, that betrayal leaves its mark. There's the emotional toll: sadness, anger, stress, fear, and irritability. But there are physical and psychological impacts as well. Psychologist Debi Silver found that more than sixty percent of the women she surveyed about betrayal suffered from low energy, extreme fatigue/exhaustion, and poor sleep.[10] More than half of them felt "overwhelmed, shocked, and unable to focus and concentrate mentally."

That sounds an awful lot like King David's state of mind and heart as he penned Psalm 55. "My thoughts trouble me and I am distraught because of what my enemy is saying," he wrote (v. 2). Fear, trembling, horror—he spilled them out on the page. It wasn't just what had been done to him, he said, it was who had done it (vs. 12-14):

If an enemy were insulting me, I could endure it; if a foe were rising against me, I could hide. But it is you, a man like myself, my companion, my close friend, with whom I

---

10. Silber, Debi. The Upside to Having Been Betrayed. *The PBT Institute.* https://pbtinstitute.com/the-upside-to-having-been-betrayed/. Retrieved February 12, 2020.

once enjoyed sweet fellowship at the house of God, as we walked about among the worshipers.

IGNORING ISSUES IS JUST STORING UP TROUBLE

Before we look more closely at David's anguish, and how he worked through it, we need to back up. Seeing how he ever came to find himself facing such heartache may provide some helpful insights for us in reducing the likelihood of similar situations.

In some ways, David was the Justin Bieber of his day—a nice-looking kid with a gift for music who almost overnight became the nation's teen pinup. His father may not have thought much of him—he didn't even mention him to Samuel the prophet, when Samuel came looking for the one to anoint as Israel's next king. However, God had already been grooming David for his future role. Out in the fields, as he watched the sheep, David grew tough and tender—he killed lions and bears that came to snatch the livestock, and he spent his free time singing songs of praise.

Before long, everyone in Israel was singing David's praises (literally)—much to the annoyance of King Saul. David "went viral" after killing Goliath and becoming Saul's military leader. Celebrating in the streets, the women sang,

"Saul has slain his thousands, and David his tens of thousands" (1 Sam. 18:7). Saul's growing insecurity forced David to run for his life, hiding out in the mountains.

God worked things deep into David's life and character during this season, for sure. But I can't help wondering whether there weren't some things that David didn't deal with—at what would later be great cost to him and others. It shouldn't be that surprising to us, really. How many times do we read of child stars whose lives end up in some sort of sad mess because they couldn't handle the freedom, the adulation, and the attention?

When everyone is telling us how great we are, it can be hard to keep the right perspective. We can be tempted to overlook what seem like small beans, because everything else is going so well. With David, the result was not uncommon for men who enjoy great success out in the world—his personal life suffered. Certainly, David found himself writing Psalm 55 because of unresolved conflict close to home.

Some people say that it all started when David stayed back instead of leading his men out to war, as he usually did. That's when he spied Bathsheba bathing, and we know how ugly that all got—adultery and murder. But, actually, the seeds of that episode were sown much earlier in his life.

In his book *Finishing Strong*, Steve Farrar observes that David was a single eighteen- or so-year-old when he was anointed king. By the time he took the throne twelve years later, he had six wives—in direct violation of God's instructions for Israel's future king according to Deuteronomy 17:17, "He must not take many wives, or his heart will be led astray." As Farrar says, "By the time David had sinned with Bathsheba he had been stretching his conscience for years." The consequences didn't end with Bathsheba getting pregnant and David arranging her husband, Uriah the Hittite's death to try to cover things up, bad as all that was. Like sin usually does, it kept rolling downhill.

Having multiple wives makes for some very complicated family dynamics. Celebrating holidays can be difficult for families these days, when there are so many divorced and remarried relatives to take into account, but those problems are nothing compared to David's. He could have done with a spreadsheet to track all his different relationships

When David was about fifty, another terrible thing happened in his life: His beautiful daughter, Tamar, was raped by her half-brother, Amnon, David's firstborn son. Rather than deal with the situation, David seems to have tried to ignore it in the hope that the problem would just disappear. We all know that doesn't work, right? Keep sweeping things under the carpet and eventually you are going to end up with a pile of dirt big enough that someone's going to trip over it.

In this case it was Absalom, Tamar's brother. He seethed quietly for two years over what Amnon had done, and finally he snapped. He went and killed Amnon. As a result, he was forced to go on the run for a couple of years. Even when David allowed Absalom to return to Jerusalem, they don't seem to have talked things out. A wedge remained between them.

Quietly, Absalom began building a following until he had enough support to launch a coup against his father. As David left his beloved city to avoid a face-to-face confrontation, he learned that this terrible family drama had taken another turn. It's one that almost sounds like it could have come out of a present-day soap opera.

Among those who went over to Absalom's side was Ahithophel, one of David's most trusted and wise counselors—who also happened to be the grandfather of Bathsheba. See how complicated this has all gotten? Did Ahithophel harbor some resentments for what had happened to Bathsheba? We tend to think of her as being equally guilty in the adultery with David, but not so fast. Since the rise of the #MeToo movement, we have become aware of how power imbalances between men in authority and women can play out, and perhaps that was part of what was going on here.

Whatever the small details, unresolved issues left David in conflict with two people who had been very close to him. They went from dear to difficult. It did not end well.

Though they were co-conspirators for a time, Absalom and Ahithophel had a falling out of their own. Not too surprising—relationships born out of a shared dislike aren't going to be healthy. Ahithophel took his own life, never seeing the grandson who might have brought him great joy, Solomon. Absalom died in the revolt at the hands of some of David's guard. What a mess.

This whole sad saga, which plays out in 2 Samuel: 13-18, is a warning for anyone in leadership today. Are there situations you are ignoring or avoiding because they seem too awkward to deal with, or because they strike too close to home? Pretending they are not there may make it feel like they have gone away for a time, but one day they are likely to "come back"—or, really, just reappear—and bite you.

So, it's all this David had in mind—broken family relationships and friendships—as he poured out his heart to God over the pain of betrayal in Psalm 55.

GETTING REAL ABOUT THE GRIEF

Learning from David may keep you from getting into a similar painful situation that could have been avoided. But it's fairly certain that at some stage you are going to find yourself experiencing the same kind of deep betrayal that He did, for one reason or another. As I noted in the introduction, Jesus couldn't have gotten to where He needed to go for us without a betrayer.

When we face our Judas, God wants to use that experience to help us fulfill His purposes for our life. David can teach us how to cooperate with that process. He may have really made some bad mistakes in his life, but he is still remembered in Scripture as a man after God's heart (1 Sam. 13:14). This is really important: We need to be sure our identity is anchored in who God says we are, not what the world says about us.

Because his heart was after God, it was soft enough to be touched. After he pursued Bathsheba and had her husband done away with, David got a visit from the prophet Nathan. The prophet spun a story about a rich man taking a poor man's one sheep, which made David mad—more evidence that, typically, he was concerned about right and wrong. In fact, David was so incensed by the injustice he heard about, he declared that the man concerned should make four-fold restitution—and in the days and years to come, David would lose four of his sons.

When the penny dropped and David realized Nathan's story was about him, he repented. From his heart poured a prayer of sorrow that is one of the most moving in the Bible. Many of us, when we have fallen, echo David's words from Psalm 51 today:

> *Have mercy on me, O God, according to your unfailing love; according to your great compassion blot out my transgressions.*

> *Wash away all my iniquity and cleanse me from my sin.*

> *For I know my transgressions, and my sin is always before me...*

> *Cleanse me with hyssop, and I will be clean; wash me, and I will be whiter than snow.*

> *Let me hear joy and gladness; let the bones you have crushed rejoice.*

Hide your face from my sins and blot out all my iniquity.

Create in me a pure heart, O God, and renew a steadfast spirit within me.

Do not cast me from your presence or take your Holy Spirit from me.

Restore to me the joy of your salvation and grant me a willing spirit, to sustain me (vs. 1-12).

David had a similar response after his betrayal by Absalom and Ahithophel—he turned his heart to God again. Having admitted his sorrow and fear and anger, he went on in Psalm 55:

As for me, I call to God, and the Lord saves me. Evening, morning and noon I cry out in distress, and he hears my voice...

Cast your cares on the Lord and he will sustain you; he will never let the righteous be shaken (vs. 16-17, 22).

David was a praying man. This wasn't a quick grace-before-meals thing. It was morning, noon, and night. He knew that he could depend on God to come through for him.

When we face betrayal, we need to acknowledge it just as David did. Sometimes, we may be tempted to think we are being spiritual by ignoring or downplaying the hurt. But that's not really faith, that's avoidance. We need to be real with God—and then we need to be ready to move on. Like David, we need to remind ourselves that God is good and to be trusted.

I wonder whether this betrayal hit David so hard because, up until this point, pretty much everything had gone his way? Yes, he had faced some hard years on the run, but even then he knew that most people were rooting for him. He had never really known defeat until the day he had to ride out of Jerusalem and hand the city over to his rebellious son.

This success seems to have blinded him to the sucker punch from someone close to him. He admitted that if this had come from an enemy, he would have known how to handle things: "If a foe were rising against me, I could hide" (Ps. 55:12). It's worth bearing in mind that if you win all the time, you won't know how to handle defeat when it finally comes one day. And it will come, that's for sure.

Participation trophies are all very well, but they aren't real life. One of the kindest things we can do for children is to teach them how to lose well!

HONORING GOD'S APPOINTED ONES

There is another lesson in David's story for dealing with difficult people. If we look at the story from the perspective of Absalom and Ahithophel, we might consider David to be the difficult person. He is the leader who in one area or another is not stepping up to the plate. What do you do in such situations?

Well, you don't go and try to overthrow God's appointed and anointed. Revolutions of that kind don't solve anything. David knew that and had lived out that principle when he was on the run from Saul, and God had honored him for it.

When I was struggling under my micromanaging, old-school senior pastor in my first church appointment I was approached by a member of the board. He said that he and some others were fed up with the way the old guy was running things too. They wanted a new pastor, and they wanted him to be me.

This kind of thing happens all the time in churches, because no leader is perfect. It's a barometer of our character: How are we going to respond when we can't control a situation to our liking? Will we give it over to God, or will we try to take matters into our own hands?

It all comes down to honor. We are called to honor people who are in authority over us—even difficult people—but this is an increasingly foreign concept in the world today. Everyone seems to be more concerned about how others treat them than they are about how they treat others. We are so busy demanding our rights that we have lost sight of our responsibilities, in some ways. This is never more true than when it comes to our parents. I tend to agree with Camryn Manheim, who said, "Parents know how to push your buttons because, hey, they sewed them on."

The Bible says we should honor our parents. It's the only one of the Ten Commandments that comes with a promise: "Honor your father and your mother, so that you may live long in the land the Lord your God is giving you" (Exod. 20:12). I can't help wondering whether the rootlessness and restlessness we see in so many young people these days, their lack of settledness, isn't somehow connected to the fact that we are not honoring our elders. In fact, a recent report in *The Washington*

Post revealed that Americans are "dying young at alarming rates."[11]

"There's something more fundamental about how people are feeling at some level—whether it's economic, whether it's stress, whether it's deterioration of family," said Ellen Meara, a professor at the Dartmouth Institute for Health Policy and Clinical Practice. "People are feeling worse about themselves and their futures, and that's leading them to do things that are self-destructive and not promoting health."

Honor is about the office God has established, not the person. You may not like the President of the United States, but you should honor the presidency. You may not like your boss, but you should honor his position. When you honor people, you don't bad-mouth them. Instead you speak blessings over them as you pray for them. In 1 Timothy 2:1-2, we are instructed to offer "petitions, prayers, intercessions, and thanksgiving… for kings and all those in authority."

I was still pretty young in my faith when I was approached to help overthrow my difficult senior pastor, but

11. Achenbach, Joe. 'There's something terribly wrong': Americans are dying young at alarming rates. https://www.washingtonpost.com/health/theres-something-terribly-wrong-americans-are-dying-young-at-alarming-rates/2019/11/25/d88b28ec-0d6a-11ea-8397-a955cd542d00_story.html. *The Washington Post*. November 26, 2019.

I knew something was off. "I'll be no part of that," I told the ringleader of the revolt. "That's who God put in charge. I'm not the guy to say he's not to be in charge. If God wants to remove the man of God, He can do so."

They went ahead with their plans, and forced a church vote over whether the pastor should go. It split the church; the pastor got the okay by just one percent, and I stayed with him. Those that wanted him out left and started a new church a ways down the road. Some of those involved in the attempt to get rid of the pastor fell on hard times. One went bankrupt, another died, a third got horribly sick. I don't believe that was all a coincidence.

I'm not saying that anyone leading a ministry gets to call all the shots, and no one can ever question them. I have seen those kinds of situations be used to cause terrible spiritual abuse. But we are called to honor our leaders and follow biblical principles. When God sets someone in place, it is not for us to "unset" them. When you choose unbiblical means, you can end up with unthinkable outcomes.

HOW TO HANDLE SNAKES

Moses is recognized as one of the greatest leaders of all time. Organizing an exodus of as many as one million people—on foot, with no cell phones or catering trucks—is no small feat. But once they were out of Egypt, some of the Israelites started to complain. They whined about Moses dragging them out into the middle of the desert and complained about the food.

They may have only been talking among themselves, but God overheard. (Keep that in mind!) He was not happy. He sent poisonous snakes into the camp, and a bunch of people died. Who did everyone turn to for help? Oh, yes, the guy who just a while ago couldn't do anything right by them. Funny how people's perceptions change when they need something.

Moses prayed, and God told him to make a snake and put it up on a pole, because anyone who had been bitten who looked at it would be spared. This wasn't just an unusual first-aid technique, it was a prophetic statement—a picture of how, in being lifted up on the cross, Jesus would deliver people from the death that can be traced back to the first serpent, Satan.

There's a lesson for us all here: When you're bitten by someone who is venomous, when their poisonous fangs sink into you, look to Jesus. When you have been bitten by a difficult person, a doctor won't be able to heal your pain.

A lawyer won't be able to heal your pain. Seeking some kind of false comfort—alcohol, pornography, shopping, whatever you may turn to—won't be able to heal your pain. Jesus can.

In His last words to His disciples, He told them that as they went out in the world in His name and power, they would be "able to handle snakes with safety" (Mark 16:18, NLT). Does that promise encourage you as you think about some people you have to deal with?

Paul knew a thing or two about dealing with poisonous types, too. On his way under guard to Rome to stand trial, the ship he was traveling on was shipwrecked on Malta. The islanders initially welcomed Paul and the other survivors, kindly building a fire because it was cold and wet. As a new leader, you may have experienced a similar warm reception. But you might have also learned that people's opinions can change quickly. They did for Paul.

As the account in Acts 28 goes on, while Paul was gathering up some sticks for the fire a deadly viper driven out by the heat struck at his hand, fastening tight. When the islanders saw this, they decided that Paul must be a murderer, because the snake bite was a sign of judgment against him. Talk about fickle.

How did Paul respond to this abrupt change in people's opinions of him? He "shook the snake off into the fire and suffered no ill effects" (v. 5). When people flip and flop over you, you need to do the same thing: Just shake it off.

You can't let the opinions of other people define who you are. "Can you believe what she said about me?" "Can you believe what he said about me?" Who cares what they said about you! Billy Graham, America's favorite preacher of the twentieth century, was once asked why he never responded to the people who were critical of him. "Answer my critics?" he responded. "My friends don't need any explanation and my critics will never believe my explanation. Why should I use my energy answering my critics?"

If someone calls you to complain, there's no need to get into a five-hour phone conversation with that person. Send a text: *Busy right now, just message me, please.* Then you have time to process and respond accordingly if you feel you need to.

What matters is not what other people say about you. What matters is what God says about you—and what you are saying about God to your situation. Just keep doing what you know to be the next right thing, and leave the rest to God. People change like the weather. Also, what are you telling your situation about God? Proverbs 18:21 says, "The tongue has the power of life and death, and those who love it will eat its fruit." What are you serving yourself?

After Paul shook that snake off everyone expected him to drop dead. "But after waiting a long time and seeing nothing unusual happen to him, they changed their minds and said he was a god" (Acts 28:6). How crazy: One minute you're the devil, the next you are Yahweh Himself. Just remember that neither is true.

FAITH OVER FEELINGS

You can't control what other people say about you, but you can choose how you let it impact you: in other words, you need to guard your ears. You also need to guide your mouth. Just as you need to be careful about what you let in, you need to be cautious about what you let out. Criticizing a critic and complaining about a complainer isn't the solution. If you keep repeating the offense to others, you are just driving that splinter deeper into your own heart and spirit. The results will not be good. Proverbs 18:19 says, "A brother wronged is more unyielding than a fortified city; disputes are like the barred gates of a citadel."

What's the answer? Look to Jesus. *Oh, come on*, you may be thinking, *give me something stronger than that!* Well, the truth is that there is nothing stronger than the name that is above every name. Turning to Him is our only hope. When everything seems hopeless, we turn to Him.

By the time he wrote Psalm 55, David had buried three sons. That's more pain than many of us will ever face, but it didn't cause him to pull away. He continued to cry out in prayer "evening, morning and noon" (v. 17). His example in this psalm is a good one. He started by pouring out his heart to God, admitting his hurt and pain. But he didn't stop there. He went on from voicing how he felt about things to declaring his belief in God's goodness.

This is an important lesson: There is a difference between our prayers and our confession of faith. Our prayers are about where we are and what we want God to do; our confession of faith is about who God is and what He has done and can do, regardless of how we feel about it.

Hebrews 13:15 says, "Through Jesus, therefore, let us continually offer to God a sacrifice of praise—the fruit of lips that openly profess His name." In the original Greek, *profess* is a compound word, *homologeo*. The first part, homo, means "the same as"—it's where we get homosapien, homogenous, homosexual. The second part is where we get logos, which means the "written word of God."

With that in mind, what rises from our lips should be the same as what God says. That's your confession of faith—that the truth about the difficult relationship you may be dealing with is not how you feel, but what God says about it. You cannot afford to give in to your emotions when you're going through a problem—whether that's a physical, financial, or relational challenge. Start putting the Word of God on the tip of your tongue. As you do, you will find the strength of God gets down deep into your soul, because God exalts His word above all things.

Remember: Praying is telling God about your situation. Your confession, or profession, of faith is telling your situation about God. When I have a problem, I start by telling God how I feel. Then I begin speaking to my problem. I tell it, "Problem, you better line up with the Word of God. I am a Word-carrying believer and God's word is all over this."

It's important to both pray and profess as a protection against a subtle secondary infection that can develop if we allow a personal betrayal to fester. Over time, we can go from just feeling let down by someone to also feeling let down by God. Why did He allow this to happen to me? Don't let that be your story.

I remember reading the story Jeremiah Johnston told in his book *Unimaginable: What Our World Would Be Like Without Christianity*, about a Christian family on their way to an evangelistic meeting. Their vehicle was hit head-on by a car being driven by a girl who was high on meth. The parents survived, but their two girls died in the wreck. What an awful thing. Though they were devastated, the parents didn't let their grief pull them under. They actually befriended the young woman who had been responsible for the accident, who went to prison and got saved while she was serving her sentence.

Contrast that with a story I came across while visiting Buenos Aires, Argentina. In the city's famous Recoleta Cemetery—said to be one of the ten most beautiful in the world—I saw the memorial to a young woman who died while on her honeymoon in Europe. The memorial includes a poem by her heartbroken father, who wrote, "I only ask myself why, if God exists, does he take away that which is not His. Because he destroys us and leaves us to an eternity of sadness! Why? I believe in fate and not in you. Why?"[12] This father lost his faith in God over the unexplainable. So sad.

You can't survive in leadership with a long list in your back pocket of people who have let you down somehow. Thankfully, God used my difficult father to teach me a lot; things that may upset other folks tend to just wash off my back. Still, I've learned as a pastor that I need to be careful to keep short accounts, or I'll will just get weighed down. If someone does get to me, I will make a point of releasing the situation and that person to the Lord. I'll tell God about the hurt, and then I will tell Him I forgive them. I pray a blessing over them and let them go. I keep praying for them until I have worked them out of my system. When is that? When they and the hurt they caused no longer keep coming to mind.

I don't want to fall into the temptation of negative thinking—either about the person, or God. Ephesians 4:27 warns "do not give the devil a foothold." Martin Luther, the father of the Reformation, once said, "You cannot keep birds from flying over your head but you can keep them from building a nest in your hair." When I am praying for a difficult

12. "Tomb of Liliana Crociati de Szaszak." *Wikipedia.com.* https://en.wikipedia.org/wiki/Tomb_of_Liliana_Crociati_de_Szaszak. Accessed March 16, 2020.

person who has wounded me, sometimes I'll lift my hands above my head as I am praying and then open them, like I am releasing a bird into the air.

Forgiveness is a verb. A verb is an action word. So when you forgive someone it's about what you do, not your emotions You don't have to feel warm and fuzzy toward that person who betrayed you, you just have to let go of the need to be proven right, the need for an apology, the need for revenge. In time, you may end up feeling warm toward him or her again, but not necessarily. You just need to be sure you're not holding on to resentment and anger.

chapter six

DEALING WITH DIFFICULT PEOPLE

EVER SINCE I said a sad goodbye to Jack the jack-ass, I've tried to have the same sort of attitude to the human Jacks I have encountered along the way. I have endeavored to be grateful for what they have brought into my life, or helped bring out of it. Like our stubborn, four-footed animal, they have turned over the ground in my heart, to help me be more fruitful. To be honest I have not shed a tear when all of them have disappeared, as I did the day Jack was taken away, but I have attempted to be thankful.

Trying to have the right attitude toward difficult people has been important. But it has not been the only principle I have learned. I have also discovered that difficult people are not all the same. Knowing their particular shades or flavors of difficulty can help you navigate them. For me, they fall into six main categories:

THE CONTROLLERS

There is only one way to do anything, whether it's leading a meeting or loading the dishwasher, and it's theirs. They have turned micromanaging into an Olympic sport. Everyone else is just plain wrong. If they are leaders, then they know that God loves you, and they have a plan for your life—in exacting detail. If they are relatives, they may insist that family gatherings always happen at a certain place and in a certain way, because that's just how it has always been done and how it will always be done, world without end, Amen.

Sometimes their tight grip is clearly evident. If they have the authority they will wield it, with detailed rules and expectations on how things should be done. If not, they will resort to passive-aggressive tactics to make sure things go their way.

This kind of definitiveness can masquerade as confidence, even arrogance. But many times it's actually disguising some kind of fear that they have. They don't trust anyone else, even God, to come through for them so they have to take control for themselves. Sadly, controllers often also justify their actions by using religious language. They insist that God says things should be this way, not that.

THE CRITICS

These folks have a slingshot hidden behind their backs. Whenever someone floats a balloon of an idea, these are the people who are all too ready to shoot it down. Rooted in the familiar, they see their job as snuffing out anything that is new or that challenges the status quo.

Oftentimes they won't come right out and be directly critical. Instead they may pretend to be positive and offer what they present as probing questions for consideration. They are just trying to help improve things! But for every proposed solution they have a multitude of problems. Having someone like this in a meeting is like driving down the freeway with the parking brake on.

Like the controllers, they can operate under the guise of faith. They may quote Proverbs 27:17 as their motivation: "As iron sharpens iron, so one person sharpens another." They pride themselves on being the one to point out the problem—it makes them feel superior to everyone else in the room. My friend Dr. Sam Chand, the leadership consultant and coach, has a great way of describing this kind of people. He likens them to those who drag a dead moose into a meeting, set it on the table and then sit back. *Okay, so now what?*

Sometimes these folks will claim they have the gift of discernment, that they are "testing the spirits," as 1 John 4:1 instructs. They may say that they are "playing devil's advocate," though really they are doing the devil's dirty work—sowing division. My opinion is that the devil already has enough people working for him; he doesn't need any more help! Instead, we need more people with God-oriented solutions.

Recently, someone on my team came to me with a problem he was facing in his department. In the middle of telling the story he suddenly stopped. "I'm sorry," he said, "I brought you a problem but no solution. I'll come back another day." That was such a blessing to me!

THE COMPLAINERS

Why waste time looking on the bright side of life when you could be grumbling about what went wrong, what is going wrong, or what could go wrong? These people never met a gift horse whose mouth they didn't want to open wide and peer down into. When they talk about their personal woes, it's in a way that leaves you feeling like somehow they are all your fault.

It's almost as though they walk around with a dark cloud over their heads—you can sense it when they come into a room. Gloom-time! They make Eeyore seem like the captain of the cheerleading squad. They have a quiet capacity for sucking the enthusiasm right out of anything.

Even if you don't take the time to respond to every complaint they have, it's like having a slow leak in your tire. Left unchecked, these Debbie Downers will have a seriously negative impact on the culture of your church, your organization, your business, or your home.

There are times when leaders need to let people go because they are messing up the culture of the organization. It's a hard thing to do, but it's one of the most rewarding. To be honest, because of my temperament I usually wait too long to show people the door because I am hoping and believing they can get better. And it's good to give people chance to grow and improve. But you need to be careful.

Let things go too long and chances are everyone else around is thinking, "Why doesn't he fire that person?" Rather than fostering an environment where people feel you are pursuing excellence, giving room for them to develop, you create a sense that mediocre is okay. I have never forgotten what one mentor told me. He had yet to find a leader who didn't say, "I wish I would have let them go sooner."

THE CROOKS

Many difficult people don't have any conscious ill-intent behind the way that they act. They don't mean to be mean, they just are. They haven't done the personal work they need to do in addressing their weaknesses and wounds. They haven't allowed God to heal and reshape them more in His image. So they end up causing problems often without even realizing it.

And then there are the people who may seem nice and helpful, but they have ulterior motives. They are not looking to give you anything—though they may pretend they want to. Really they are out to get something to their advantage: a position, influence, acceptance, money. They are drawn to churches like bees to honey, because they know they are going to find sympathetic, welcoming, and sometimes just too-gullible people.

Crooks can cause real havoc. I remember Dr. Michael Maiden, a pastor-friend whose growing church collapsed after it was discovered that the treasurer had embezzled millions of dollars gathered through what turned out to be a Ponzi scheme. Michael finally saw his shredded ministry and reputation restored, but not before enduring a long season of suffering and struggle. If you think you've had it bad, read his inspiring story in *God of the Comeback: It's Never Too Late.*

I'm not suggesting we have to view everyone as a potential trickster. There is a difference between being cautious and being suspicious. In our organization we say that we trust people, but we also verify. If you want to work for us, we are going to run all the checks possible. If you want to do business with us, we're going to get a couple of other bids. That's not being cynical, it's being wise as serpents, like Jesus encouraged (Matt. 10:16).

THE CONFLICTED

Some people do seem to have been dealt a harder hand in the card game of life than others, don't they? Maybe it's physical limitations or challenges, or they have endured a terrible upbringing that has left them emotionally scarred. Perhaps they are under spiritual attack beyond anything they have had to handle before. They are genuinely needy… but, boy, can they wear you down. They end up sucking the life out of you and everyone else.

Now, there's no shame in being in need and being weak. That's why God gave us to each other to care for, in the church. It's when those things become someone's identity and he or she can see no hope for a better future, that it starts to get difficult. There comes a time when we start having to take some responsibility for ourselves and our situation. For example, at Visalia First, people know we will help them out financially a time or two, but that's not our long-term responsibility—we are not a godly ATM. When the same people turn up at church every week with a different need—the rent's overdue, the car needs fixing, a dental cavity has to be filled—it can get draining.

Paul wouldn't have had to warn us to "not become weary in doing good" (Gal. 6:9) if he hadn't known that it was a real danger.

THE CO-OPTED

Sometimes, difficult people aren't just driven by their own shadows. On occasion they are in the grip of something deeper, which is simply beyond their ability to handle—maybe an addiction of some kind, or a psychological condition, or physical limitation, or mental illness.

And then there are some who may be used by darkness itself, by the devil. I'm not saying that he is pulling the strings behind every difficult person you will deal with—though he will certainly try to take advantage of any human-based conflict or problem that may arise. He is a great opportunist.

However, there are times when he will directly work to get people to try to thwart the purposes of God, whether they are aware of it or not. The devil entered Judas, who then went looking for a way to betray Jesus (Luke 22:3-4). When Paul was evangelizing in Philippi, a slave girl afflicted by a spirit kept interrupting him and distracting him before he finally cast it out of her.

Don't be intimidated when you discern the hand of the enemy in a difficult-person situation. In fact, you should be encouraged. First, you must be doing something right for the devil to want to work so hard to stop you. And, then, remember that he thought he was using Judas to stop Jesus in His ministry, but he was actually only setting things up for His ultimate and eternal victory.

HOW TO AVOID DIFFICULT PEOPLE

As I learned from my father, it's important to know which battles to fight and which ones to let go. For leaders, difficult people should be a team sport as much as possible. I mean, it's not your role to handle every single difficult person that comes along, just because you may be the target by virtue of your position and visibility.

At Visalia First, I am shielded from a lot of unnecessary interaction with difficult people. We have two boards which, like in football, run interference for me. It's like I get to play quarterback, concentrating on my throw knowing I am in a safe pocket that is protecting me from hits. The boards handle situations where they can tell people that we have policies regarding this issue or that situation. This makes any conflict less of a personal thing. If people get mad for any reason, it isn't so much at me personally, as the church.

Apart from anything, this frees the leader up to focus more on what he or she should be doing—leading. This is straight out of Moses' play-book. After he had led the people of God out of slavery in Egypt, he found himself getting worn out trying to handle all their little disputes. He talked it over with his father-in-law, Jethro, who had some wise counsel (Exodus 18:17-23):

> *What you are doing is not good. You and these people who come to you will only wear yourselves out. The work is too heavy for you; you cannot handle it alone. Listen now to me and I will give you some advice, and may God*

be with you. You must be the people's representative be-
fore God and bring their disputes to him. Teach them his
decrees and instructions, and show them the way they
are to live and how they are to behave. But select capa-
ble men from all the people—men who fear God, trust-
worthy men who hate dishonest gain—and appoint them
as officials over thousands, hundreds, fifties and tens.
Have them serve as judges for the people at all times, but
have them bring every difficult case to you; the simple
cases they can decide themselves. That will make your
load lighter, because they will share it with you. If you do
this and God so commands, you will be able to stand the
strain, and all these people will go home satisfied.

They did the same thing when life started to get hectic
in the early church. As numbers grew, it became clear that
someone needed to pay attention to how to best care for
some of the members who were in need. The disciples got
together and decided (Acts 6:2-4):

It would not be right for us to neglect the ministry of the
word of God in order to wait on tables. Brothers and sis-
ters, choose seven men from among you who are known
to be full of the Spirit and wisdom. We will turn this

responsibility over to them and will give our attention to prayer and the ministry of the word.

HOW TO MINIMIZE DIFFICULT PEOPLE

Even with a good team around you to keep unnecessary problem people at bay, there will be times when you find yourself facing a challenging person. Still, not all of them have to escalate to the status of difficult. Just because they have knocked on your door does not mean that you have to let them in. You probably have a peephole there. If so, quietly look through it and decide whether this is someone you should open the door to. As someone said, "I don't have to attend every argument I'm invited to."

We need to reevaluate the basis on which we decide whether people are difficult or not. Many times it's because of how they make us feel, but our emotions are not always the best barometer. John Joliffe, a friend and wise therapist, helped me understand this. From his professional life, which includes more than a decade hosting a live, daily therapy call-in show on the radio, he has learned how to stop difficult people from getting to him. He provides a solution that will stop difficult people and situations from getting the upper hand.

He says that life boils down to some basic ABCs:

A. The *events* of everyday life.

B. How we *evaluate* these events; what we tell ourselves about them.

C. The feelings or *emotions* that rise up in us as a result.

There's not much we can do about the As of life unless we decide to stay in bed with the blankets over our heads. Stuff, as the saying goes, is going to happen—a million times a day. Birds are going to fly over your head. The price of a cup of your favorite coffee is going to go up. Someone is going to cut you off in traffic on the way to work.

Most of us just jump to the Cs next, thinking they are caused by the As. You worry about getting pooped on. You fret over whether you're going to have to switch to a cheaper blend. You hit the horn and mouth a word or two of advice at the careless motorist. You accept that your reaction is because of what happened. That leaves us all at the mercy of a world beyond our control.

But the reality is, we are missing an important split second between A and C. It's in the Bs, our self-talk about what the As mean, that we actually determine whether or not we will be scared, frustrated, or hostile. That's because the Cs are the by-products of our inner self-counsel.

That may sound daunting, but it is actually very liberating. Because it means we have the power to respond differently. We don't have to let the As dictate the way our lives go. The problem is not the problem—the problem is what we think about the problem. If we can change our thoughts, we can change our feelings about situations—and people.

John's idea, that the way we believe things are may not actually be the way they really are, is supported by the Bible. In 2 Corinthians 10:5, Paul writes about how believers should "take captive every thought to make it obedient to Christ." It's a way to "demolish arguments and every pretension that sets itself up against the knowledge of God," he says—that is, the truth.

This can be learned, but it may take some time to develop new memory muscle (not muscle memory!). After all, you are unlearning the reactive habit of a lifetime. It can be done, though. Try it in the coming week. Think of three recent situations or events and write down the ABC of each. You will start to identify where your instinctual thinking may have led to you feeling a certain way about something. Take some time to evaluate how accurate that thinking was—whether it lined up with what you know to be true, or what you know God's truth to be.

Over time, you will find that the way you respond to some of your As will change. Understanding more about the situation or the person involved may result in you changing the way you think about it or them. In turn, you don't find yourself flooded with extreme emotions. You can recognize that an emergency on someone else's part doesn't have to be an emergency on yours. That problem still needs to be dealt with, but it no longer qualifies as a crisis. You still have to interact with that problem person, but they no longer qualify as an out-and-out difficult person.

HOW TO HANDLE DIFFICULT PEOPLE

Your best efforts aren't going to make your life a difficult-person-free-zone. They are out there, and you are going to have to deal with them. But having reduced their frequency by avoiding them where possible, and downgrading their impact on you where appropriate, you will have more emotional and spiritual capacity to face those you must. It's all in your hands. Or hand.

When we meet someone, we will often shake his or her hand. So next time you find yourself having to deal with a difficult person, imagine that you are going to reach out your hand to greet them with a shake, and let its five parts be a simple guide.

The *index finger* has great power; think about how it points the way. The rest of our body follows the lead of this one digit. In that way it's a reminder of our tongue, because what we say—to ourselves and others—points the way that the rest of us will follow.

So the first thing to do when a difficult person comes into your life is to speak life. Proverbs 18:21 says, "The tongue has the power of life and death." If you woke up this morning and the first thing that went through your mind about that difficult person was that you wanted to scratch their eyes out, reverse the talk. Say a prayer for or a blessing over them—out loud. There is something about doing so audibly that makes it more real.

The *middle finger* usually stands up taller than all the others, and in that way it symbolizes our talents—those things that make us stand out from the rest. Take that gifting or ability and put it to use in service to someone else. According to Proverbs 16:27 (TLB), "Idle hands are the devil's workshop." If you are busy using your hands to help someone else, you are less likely to be thinking how you'd like to wrap them around a certain someone's neck.

One thing about using our gifts—though they may make us stand out—is that we don't need to draw attention to ourselves. There's an important lesson for us all in Jesus's first miracle, when he turned the water into wine at the wedding in Cana. Only those behind the scenes knew there was a miracle; everyone else just thought that the bridegroom had saved the best wine until last. In the same way, if we can busy ourselves with serving—and not fretting about that difficult person, or receiving any credit for what we are doing—we may get to be part of God's doing amazing things.

The *ring finger* represents our thoughts. It's where the wedding band goes, a reminder of how important it is to be careful to guard our thinking because, as I mentioned a while back, it fuels our emotions. Don't keep going over in your mind what that person said or did. Philippians 4:8 says, "Whatever is true, whatever is noble, whatever is right, whatever is pure, whatever is lovely, whatever is ad-mirable—if anything is excellent or praiseworthy—think about such things."

To emphasize how important this is, take a moment to try to wiggle your ring finger without moving the others. Can't do it, right? That is why we need to be diligent about watching what we let our minds dwell on. Proverbs 4:23 says, "Above all else, guard your heart, for everything you do flows from it."

I actually wrote a whole book about this important principle, *Mind Viruses*. It is based on seven simple words that can change your life: As you think, so shall you be. Have you ever wondered why successful people are successful? It is because that is what they focus their thinking on. Have you ever wondered too why some people are broke all the time? It is evident in the way they think.

The *pinkie* may not look like much, but it is more important than you may be aware. Without it, you lose a lot of your hand strength. And without it, some say, your balance isn't as good. In the same way, what you do with your time will have a big effect on the rest of your life. Are you using that free time of yours in constructive ways—building healthy relationships with others, pursuing your own intimacy with God, serving others? Or are you lying around at home feeding your negativity online and from the television?

The *thumb* is what sets us apart from most of the rest of creation. Its opposability has enabled us as humans to create amazing works of art and incredible machinery. As such, you might call it the source of our treasure. The thumb is also far stronger than the fingers, capable of punching through things they can't. Ever had trouble piercing a sealed medicine container? Your thumb probably came to the rescue.

In dealing with my share of difficult people, I have often found that my treasure has given me a breakthrough where other efforts have failed. Specifically, I mean giving it away—whether that's actual cash or possessions.

One time I was having a problem getting over my dealings with a really difficult woman, and I felt God told me to give a sizable financial gift to a female missionary. I did so, and my frustration and resentment with that other person melted away. I have also given away seven vehicles over the years, as a way of making sure that greed and selfishness— me, me, me—don't get a grip on my life.

I am not sure all together how this works, but it does. Jesus said that "where your treasure is, there your heart will be also" (Matt. 6:21), so that surely has something to do with it. He also gave a pointed warning in Luke 12:15, "Watch out! Be on your guard against all kinds of greed; life does not consist in an abundance of possessions." Perhaps by giving to bless other people I am helping turn my heart away from negativity to and grumbling about others. All I know is that it works: somehow being generous loosens the grip that resentment and grievance can have on me.

My giving is the only proof that greed has not mastered me. If someone comes to me having a problem forgiving another person or getting over some kind of an offense, or even struggling with forgiving themselves for some big sin they still feel bad about, I will often prescribe their giving something they value away. Guilt offerings were a common practice in Old Testament life, and while we don't live under the law any more, sometimes when we do something in the material world, that action helps it somehow become real to us in the spiritual world.

The same kind of principle can work in dealing with difficult people. If they are short and sharp with us, rather than fight fire with fire and be snappy in return, we can be gentle and patient. Where people are suspicious, we offer trust. When people tear down, we build up. This kind of counter-intuitive response is sometimes known as responding in the opposite spirit. Jesus instructed His disciples in this approach when He commissioned them for their first mission trips: "I am sending you out like sheep among wolves" (Matt. 10:16).

St. Francis of Assisi captured the idea famously in his prayer:

Lord, make me an instrument of your peace; where there is hatred, let me sow love; where there is injury, pardon; where there is discord, union; where there is doubt, faith;

where there is despair, hope; where there is darkness, light; and where there is sadness, joy.

HOW TO SURVIVE A DIFFICULT PERSON ENCOUNTER

I've had many face-to-face encounters with difficult people through my years as a pastor. I'm a peaceable guy by nature, so I still don't find them easy, but I know they sometimes have to happen. Thankfully, Jesus gave clear directions on how to deal with difficult people in Matthew 18. When I am preparing for a difficult conversation with a difficult person, I try to remind myself of these seven principles.

Be discerning. We need to ask for God's wisdom to understand what drives them to be the way they are. As I have mentioned, in 1 John 4:1 we are cautioned to "test the spirits." Ask yourself whether this conflict or issue is a hill you really need to die on. If there is an important issue at stake, can you meet their need or concern in some way without capitulating? Learn to negotiate through some give and take. Make it a win-win rather than a win-lose, if you can.

Be attentive. Try to emulate St. Francis of Assisi, who prayed "not so much to be understood as to understand." It's been said that because we have two ears and one mouth, we should do twice as much listening as talking, and that's still true. Listen to what people are really saying. While they talk about one thing, the real issue could be something else completely. And, many times, people say more with their tone of voice or their body language than they do with their actual words.

Be cautious. We can be all too quick to rush to judgment about someone without knowing their situation and circumstances. Maybe that grumpy person is tired from caring for a sick relative, or struggling because of some other undisclosed hardship. There is a bit of a dispute over who it should actually be credited to, but there's that famous saying, "Be kind, for everyone you meet is fighting a hard battle." If you haven't walked in their shoes, you may not know what causes them to limp or stumble. James 1:19 says, "Everyone should be quick to listen, slow to speak and slow to become angry." Og Mandino said, "Treat everyone you meet as if they were going to be dead at midnight. Extend them all the care, kindness and understanding you can muster. Your life will never be the same."

Be humble. Check your ego at the door. There is often some small element of truth in even the most extreme criticism. Your posture can affect theirs. If you go in showing openness and willingness to learn, they may respond in like manner. Proverbs 15:1 says, "A gentle answer turns away wrath, but a harsh word stirs up anger." Commit to responding to what they say, rather than reacting.

Be proactive. Look for ways to accommodate them without surrendering. If you need to say sorry, seek some way to turn that into concrete action that they will remember. And if you say you are going to do something, be sure to do it. Demonstrate you are not just paying them lip service, but follow through. The quicker the better—seize the moment of agreement or reconciliation and then move on.

Be firm. At the end of the day, you may need to tell them no, or to give them clear direction they don't like. You might have to challenge their behavior and tell them they need to stop treating you unfairly. If so, be unapologetic, be unambiguous, and be uncompromising. It's okay to stand your ground if you have first knelt before God. The older I get, the more I find myself saying no than yes. I no longer feel the need to say yes to every request or opportunity.

Be peaceful. Difficult people are draining. After you've had an encounter with one, be kind to yourself. Take time to debrief: Review your interaction and evaluate how you handled the situation. Then de-stress: Go for a walk, take in a movie, whatever. Give your heart and your brain some space to recover. Accept the limitations of living in a fallen world. At the end of the day, Romans 12:18 says, "If it is possible, as far as it depends on you, live at peace with everyone." That suggests Paul knew hunky-dory wasn't always going to be in the cards.

By definition, leading or living with difficult people is never easy. But, then, no one ever said it was! Though it's no fun, dealing with them well can be a blessing in disguise, as it helps shape you more into the follower and leader God wants you to be—more compassionate, more confident, more courageous, more like Jesus.

chapter seven

THE POWER TO LOVE

SO THIS GUY went for an interview for a job as a lumberjack, the story goes. He impressed the man in the hiring department with his knowledge about all kinds of trees and how to deal with them. He seemed to be a shoo-in for the gig. But first, he was told, there had to be a trial run. The guy was given a chainsaw and told he had three attempts in which to prove he could meet the daily requirement of twenty trees felled.

The next day, the guy went out into the woods with a confident stride. At the end of the day he returned sweaty and a bit discouraged-looking, having cut down only eight trees. Never mind, the hiring guy told him, you've got another chance tomorrow.

The guy was there bright and early the following day. By the end of the shift he was tired, and had managed to add only four more trees to his previous total. Down but determined, he went home to rest up and come back for his final big push.

At the end of his third trial day, the guy dragged himself into the hiring man's office and collapsed into a chair. He dropped the chainsaw on the floor and told the man he had tried his absolute best, but still only managed to cut down eighteen trees, still short of the goal.

The hiring man said that he was sorry, but there was no job. However, by way of some consolation he would pay the candidate for his three days' work, after he had checked the chainsaw.

The hiring man got up from behind his desk, came round and picked up the chainsaw. He pulled the cord, at which the chainsaw coughed to life—and the job seeker jumped out of his seat in surprise. "Yikes!" he cried, "what's that?"

The moral of the story is probably clear. You can know exactly what you should do and give it your best shot, but without accessing the power that is available to you, there's no way you can be successful in your own strength.

If that's true for chopping down trees, then it is even more true when it comes to dealing with difficult people. All the insight and understanding in the world, all your best efforts to be kind and caring and calm and clear, aren't going to cut it! You need to tap into a power that is beyond your own abilities.

We are talking about something supernatural. Loving people the way God does. And we tend to forget how radically different that is to our human nature.

JOIN THE REVOLUTION

Jesus turned things upside down from the get-go. His first big public appearance after choosing His twelve disciples was to preach what became known as the Sermon on the Mount to a large crowd on the side of a hill. He didn't waste any time in getting down to business. If this was the opening day of His new Bible school, then this particular message was the core curriculum His students would be learning in the rest of their studies. This may have been a freshman crowd, but He was giving an advanced class.

He began by upsetting the typical religious thinking of the day, which was that if you were better off, it must mean that you were a better person. No way. God was close to the poor, the hungry, and the hated, He said. As for those who had it all, their time was coming.

What came next? He told the crowd (Luke 6:27-36):

But to you who are listening I say: Love your enemies, do good to those who hate you, bless those who curse you, pray for those who mistreat you. If someone slaps you on one cheek, turn to them the other also. If someone takes your coat, do not withhold your shirt from them. Give to everyone who asks you, and if anyone takes what belongs to you, do not demand it back. Do to others as you would have them do to you. If you love those who love you, what credit is that to you? Even sinners love those who love them. And if you do good to those who are good to you, what credit is that to you? Even sinners do that. And if you lend to those from whom you expect repayment, what credit is that to you? Even sinners lend to sinners, expecting to be repaid in full. But love your enemies, do good to them, and lend to them without expecting to get anything back. Then your reward will be great, and you will be children of the Most High, because he is kind to the ungrateful and wicked. Be merciful, just as your Father is merciful.

Some of us have read and heard these words so often they are very familiar to us. As a result we don't get how shocking, even offensive, they were to Jesus' audience back then. Love your enemies. Seriously? Do good to those who hate you. Really? Pray for those who mistreat you. Come on, now!

Those hearing Jesus' words weren't just thinking about the falling out they may have had with a neighbor or a squabble with a distant relative. Their minds must have immediately gone to the Romans under whose occupation they were living.

To most Jews, the Romans were tyrants and terrorists. They hadn't gotten to conquer much of the known world by being nice and handing out candies. They did so with an iron fist. They levied heavy taxes, and soldiers could require anyone to carry a load for them like a servant. No wonder many Jews thought back to the Maccabean revolt against the Seleucid Greeks almost two hundred years earlier and wished for a similar uprising.

Even those who didn't want to go crazy against their oppressors were looking for some sort of retribution. They expected to get their pound of flesh, one day. After all, in the Old Testament, Moses had laid down the law of an eye for an eye and a tooth for a tooth. It was the flip-side of you scratch my back, I'll scratch yours. You scratch one of my eyes out, and I get to scratch one of yours out in return to balance things out.

So, the Jews were looking for a revolution, and Jesus gave them one—only not the kind they were hoping for. Here He came telling them to love their enemies. Really? It's hard enough to love our family and friends, sometimes!

Now, to be able to grasp what Jesus was saying, we need to recognize that we use the word *love* imprecisely, in the same way that we do the word relationships, as I mentioned earlier. Take me as an example. I love my wife. I love my dog. I love ice cream. The intensity of my feelings toward each of those and my level of commitment to them are not the same, however! The same word is used for very different degrees of passion.

We need to turn to the Greek language used in the writing of the New Testament to do justice to the word, and to find the help we need to truly love difficult people. When we read about love there, it could be one of four different Greek words: *phileo, storge, eros,* or *agape.* C.S. Lewis wrote about them and the differences between them in his famous book, *The Four Loves.* Remarkably, they were a feature of the 2020 Super Bowl.

Like many people, I watch the biggest event of the football year on television as much for the adverts as the game itself. Businesses pull out all the stops for their slots, which can cost several million dollars. Some of the ads are hilarious; some are hair-raising. All of them aim to make a big impact.

So I was astonished by New York Life Insurance's low-key, sixty-second spot during the clash between the San Francisco 49ers and the Kansas City Chiefs. "Love in Action,"[13] as it was called, opened with the narrator declaring, "The ancient Greeks had four words for love." It then went on to describe each briefly, over footage capturing the different kinds—friends, siblings playing together, a romantic couple, parents and their children, caregivers.

"The fourth kind of love is different," the narrator said. "It's the most admirable. It's called agape: love as an action. It takes courage. Sacrifice. Strength. For 175 years, we've been helping people act on their love so they can look back or look ahead and say: We got it right. We did good."

Wow! Who would have expected a lesson about God's love in the middle of the big game? Because, although the makers didn't quote the Bible directly that's in effect what

13. https://www.youtube.com/watch?v=-3LTR32dMgI

they were presenting. Let's look a little more closely at each of those four kinds of love.

PHILEO: BROTHERLY LOVE

This is the most common form of love. It has the meaning of "to approve of, to like, to treat affectionately or kindly." It's about friendship. *Phileo* is the root of Philadelphia, which of course is known as the city of brotherly love.

Lewis described *phileo* as the "humblest love." Saying it is the most basic form of love is not playing it down, however. We all need to experience this kind of love. What may start as a casual connection can grow into one of those friends-for-a-lifetime relationships we all need.

As I have mentioned, I have some friends I made in college who remain close to this day. Any of us can call and ask to meet somewhere in a few days' time and, as far as is possible, we'll all be there. We hang out and let our guards down in a no-judgment zone. And we have fun together.

Being with these friends makes me think of the movie *The Legend of Bagger Vance*. In the title role as the messenger sent to help a former top golfer who has lost his swing, Will Smith declares, "God is happiest when He looks down and sees His kids at play." I'm convinced today more than ever that we are meant to enjoy life, not just endure it. Find some friends to do life with, and enjoy it!

STORGE: FAMILY LOVE

This refers to a natural or instinctive kind of love that just is, often because of some kind of family connection. It's the source of the saying that blood is thicker than water. As I have said, I see this more clearly in some communities than others, where family bonds remain strong.

Family can be the source of some of our greatest frustrations and hurts, of course, but it is also where we can know we are accepted come what may. Robert Frost, the famous poet, said, "Home is the place where, when you have to go there, they have to take you in."

Mom taught me about this in buckets. Life can't have been easy married to Dad, but she never complained to us or let on. She loved us kids fiercely—with an emphasis on the fierce, at times! She chased one of my brothers three blocks, on one occasion, to be sure he got a good whipping for some infraction. But we knew that she loved us.

She made sure I went to Sunday School every week, so I would be in an environment where I might hear something about God. And when I got too big to be ordered to go, and stayed home lying in bed on Sunday mornings, she would leave the television on loud. She tuned it in to a station that broadcast services by a preacher who had a pretty daughter with a sweet voice, both of which Mom knew might get me to listen in.

EROS: ROMANTIC LOVE

This is the kind that gets all the press! From it we get *erotic* and *eroticism*. Actually, the word itself does not appear in the New Testament. (It's not in the Old Testament either, because that was written in Hebrew, not Greek.) That's not to say that you can't find its flavor in the Bible, like salt on a good meal.

To get a glimpse, go read the Song of Solomon. Oh, my. It's all perfume and wine and kisses. She's likened to a mare, while he's a stag. She is "faint with love," while he praises her "delights." Somebody get them a room!

Clearly, the Bible doesn't just condone sexual attraction, it celebrates it—in the right context of a covenant relationship. The sad thing is that this amazing gift has been distorted and devalued by the world. It's become an exchange rather than a commitment. It's used to sell everything from cosmetics to cars.

AGAPE: SELFLESS LOVE

As that New York Life ad noted, the last kind of love is different. It is also the one Jesus had in mind when He spoke of loving our enemies, or difficult people.

The other three kinds of love come from within us, in different ways. *Agape* comes from God. It's unconditional, undeserved. It's nothing about the recipient—they can't earn or deserve it in any way. It's all about the giver. And, as 1 John 4:8 says, "God *is* love" (emphasis added). Not that He has some love to share, but it is His very essence, the core of who He is. The root word here for God's love-nature is *agape*, which means "to wish well, to take pleasure in, to long for."

We simply don't have it in us to act like this toward other people, at least not always. Sure, we can be loving to those who love us; Jesus acknowledged that in His sermon. However, even with those who are nearest and dearest to us there will be times when we wonder whatever we saw in them.

Only when we have experienced something of God's *agape* love toward us can we begin to be a conduit of it to others.

When I got saved, it was a dramatic turnaround. At nineteen, I was going nowhere, a party waiting to happen, always ready to smoke some weed or chug some alcohol. When someone invited me to a church service I only agreed to go because they said there would be some girls there. Instead, I met the Holy Spirit when some of the people there prayed for me. It was a powerful experience: I quit four major habits overnight. No more getting high, no more getting drunk, no more smoking, no more cussing, My appetite for those things disappeared just like that.

In their place I had this passion for God. I immediately began telling my friends about Jesus. I just wanted them to encounter the Holy Spirit like I had. But there was part of me that was very black-and-white about things, maybe because my experience had been so dramatic. Although I knew God had forgiven me all my sins, I had a sneaking feeling that if I ever ran into Him, the number one thing on His agenda would be my sinful ways, not His love for me.

About a month after my conversion, I was at a family gathering at Lake O' the Pines in East Texas. My oldest brother, Johnny, and I took a canoe out on the water and it capsized. Somehow I got knocked unconscious as we flipped.

The next thing I knew I was having a near-death experience, watching from outside myself as my body sank in the deep water. Dirty as it was, the water was illuminated by some sort of incredible light, and I was filled with an indescribable sense of love and peace and joy. No strings attached, just complete acceptance. Though Dad may have been mean to me, I always knew that Mom loved me, and my siblings did, but this feeling was like nothing I had ever known. I was overwhelmed by an awareness that God was good, and He loved me completely. I didn't want it to end. Dying didn't seem so bad.

As my body kept sinking, suddenly two guys appeared out of nowhere and pulled me to the surface. Somehow I was dragged to the shore, where people gathered around my apparently lifeless body. Johnny was sure I was a goner. He was crying and saying how sorry he was for not having been a better brother to me.

They carried me back semi-conscious to where we were staying. I asked who had dragged me to the shore, and no one seemed to know. *What had happened to the two guys that pulled me up from the bottom of the lake?* I asked. *What two guys?* everyone asked me. They hadn't seen anyone.

I have no doubt that God sent two angels that day to yank me out of the water. Since then I have had no fear of death; I know without a shadow of a doubt that, for those who love God, what is on the other side is so amazing it makes being here on earth pale in comparison. In fact, I later did some research into near-death experiences and spoke with a number of people who had gone through something like what I did. I wrote about all that in my book, *I Shook Hands With Death*. All but one of them said that, like me, they were reluctant to come back.

That event did more than just give me a hunger for heaven. It also left me with a greater awareness of God's great love for everyone here on earth. I have never quite experienced again the intensity of it like I did that day in the lake, when it felt as though I was drowning in His love rather than water, but I have carried with me a greater sense of His *agape* love that has helped me when dealing with difficult people. When you realize that the end of the world isn't the end of the world, having peo-ple hurt you and let you down no longer feels like the end of the world.

Many people have told me that I am too kind to peo-ple that work for me. If so, I think it stems back to my experience in the lake that day. I was so touched by God's *agape* love that it became an intrinsic part of me. I truly believe that there is good in everyone, and if I am having difficulty with anyone I will attempt to find that good and nourish it.

GROWING INTO AGAPE LOVE

We don't all get the sort of opportunity I did to encounter *agape* love like that, of course. Maybe most people don't need it like I did. Sometimes it's a more gradual experience of more and more of God's love, as we grow in faith over time. For some, it may come through another person who just exudes it. I had a professor like that when I was in seminary, Dr. Roy Fish, who took me back a bit to Lake O' the Pines. God's love seemed to just beam out of him like sunshine. I hope you meet someone like Dr. Fish or have an experience similar to mine, to experience a love that goes so deep. It's a game-changer.

When you are so full of God's love that not much else really matters, it's easier to be forgiving toward difficult people. This is a process for all of us. One of the neat things about God is that He is patient with us, working with our limitations. He comes down to our level, so that He can then lift us up to His. That's the gospel message in a nutshell, isn't it?

We see it played out in regard to loving people in Jesus' relationship with Peter. After He had risen from the dead, Jesus had that encounter with Peter on the seashore (John

21). Over breakfast He asked Peter three times whether he loved Him—once for each occasion Peter had denied Jesus the night He was arrested. Jesus wanted Peter to be completely free of any lingering sense of failure and regret. He would need to be for all that was to come.

On the first occasion Jesus asked Peter (v. 15), "Do you love [*agape*] me more than these?"

Peter's response is telling. "Yes, Lord," he said, "you know that I love [*phileo*] you."

Despite all the incredible things he had witnessed and experienced in his time following Jesus, Peter still had an earthbound, man-sized love for Him.

So Jesus asked again, with the same response. His *agape* for Peter's *phileo* (v. 16).

The next go-round, Jesus adjusted (v. 17):

The third time He said to him, "Simon son of John, do you love [phileo] me?"

Peter was hurt because Jesus asked him the third time, "Do you love [phileo] me?" He said, "Lord, you know all things; you know that I love [phileo] you."

Jesus met Peter where he was, but He didn't leave him there. Over time, Peter grew in his understanding, experience, and expression of God's love. Initially, he focused on sharing the gospel with other Jews. When he had a vision in which he was instructed to eat animals considered unclean under Jewish law, he refused. Only after God spoke to him again did he change his mind.

The account in Acts 10 goes on to describe how Peter then went on to share the gospel with Gentiles for the first time. "I now realize how true it is that God does not show favoritism but accepts from every nation the one who fears Him and does what is right," he declared (vs. 34-35).

Peter's heart seems to have continued to soften and broaden over the years. I'm reminded of the saying that when God stretches us, it's so that He can occupy a larger space. That appears to have been the case with Peter. By the time he wrote the letters that he contributed to the New Testament, he had been elevated in his understanding and experience of God's love.

In 1 Peter 4:8, he wrote, "Above all, love [*agape*] each other deeply, because love [*agape*] covers over a multitude of sins." Only *agape*—not *phileo,* not *storge,* not *eros*—could do that! Signing off in the next chapter (5:14), he wrote, "Greet one another with a kiss of love [*agape*]." Note he had gone from *phileo* to *agape*.

Peter demonstrated what his fellow apostle wrote in 1 John 4:17, "As we live in God, our love grows more perfect." Our job is to cooperate with Him in that.

I've come a long way through the years, but I have certainly not arrived yet. Just the other day, I had an accident in my car and needed to take it to the repair shop. When I picked it up I could tell there was still something wrong, so I took it back. I ended up having to go back with it five times, and I was not happy, to say the least.

It was a reminder of an uncomfortable truth about dealing with difficult people—that the most difficult person we will ever have to deal with in our lives may well be ourselves. As the saying goes, "We have met the enemy, and he is us."

I don't know about you, but I still need some more perfecting. There are times when, because I fall short, I am another's difficult person. Like my car, I need to keep having to go back to the manufacturer—in my case, God. I need to keep being renewed by and filled with His *agape* love.

What does it look like to love others the way that God loves us? Well, it means being nice to them whether they deserve it or not. In the Sermon on the Mount, Jesus said that "God is kind to ungrateful and wicked people" (Luke

6:35). It also means forgiving them, just as Jesus did when He hung on the cross. "Father, forgive them, for they do not know what they are doing," He said (Luke 23:24).

He didn't mean that literally. He wasn't saying they were in a trance or that they had been tricked somehow; they were aware of what they were doing. They just didn't realize the full significance of their actions. In the same way, some of the difficult people we have to deal with know exactly the actions they are taking and the things they are saying; they are not an accident. But we need to acknowledge they may not fully realize the consequences, or that the devil is using them to hate the God inside of us.

What sets *agape* love apart from the three others— *phileo*, *storge*, *eros*—is that it is not based on feelings. The three involve us feeling something: friendly, family, or frisky. *Agape* is all about God and His actions for and in us. It's love as a verb.

That is why Jesus could say, "A new *command* I give you: Love one another. As I have loved you, so you must love one another" (John 13:34, emphasis added). Jesus wasn't being unrealistic here. You can't summon feelings of affection on demand; it's just not possible. But you can choose to act lovingly toward people—that is, in their best interests.

And, many times, in due course the feelings will follow. But even if they don't we are to *agape*.

This was a stretch for the disciples, when they first heard it. Peter went to Jesus and wanted to know just how far this forgiving people thing was supposed to go; maybe seven times, he wondered? No, Jesus told him, seventy times seven (That's 490, in case you weren't sure!) (Matt. 18:22, NKJV). In another account of that exchange, the reaction of the disciples shows just how humanly unreasonable this was. "Increase our faith!" they cried (Luke 17:5).

However, it is important to remember that God doesn't ask things of us that are impossible with His help. He has never said to me, "Mike, today I want you to be Asian." I just don't have it in me—literally. But when He commands us to love and forgive people—including the unlovable and the downright difficult—it is because He has given us the capacity to do so, through His Holy Spirit in us.

When we live and move in God's *agape* love, as difficult people come into our lives, we can, like Jesus, say "Friend," knowing that they are part of our journey to our destiny.

As I was finishing work on this book, I got a call about another tragedy. A young baby had drowned in a swimming pool.

"How do you explain this?" one of our parishioners asked.

"I can't," I answered. "But the real question in life is not why do bad things happen to good people. The real question of life is what do good people do when bad things happen?"

So what are you going to do about that difficult person in your life? Are you going to rise above the situation? Will you dig deep into God's love and allow Him to perfect you in the process? I pray for you that the latter occurs.

Heaven is next. I'll see you there!

NOTES